On Teaching and Learning

On Teaching and Learning

Putting the Principles and Practices of Dialogue Education into Action

Jane Vella

Foreword by Joanna Ashworth

JOSSEY-BASS
A Wiley Imprint
www.josseybass.com

Published by Jossey-Bass
A Wiley Imprint
989 Market Street, San Francisco, CA 94103-1741—www.josseybass.com

Jossey-Bass books and products are available through most bookstores. To contact Jossey-Bass directly call our Customer Care Department within the U.S. at 800-956-7739, outside the U.S. at 317-572-3986, or fax 317-572-4002.

Jossey-Bass also publishes its books in a variety of electronic formats. Some content that appears in print may not be available in electronic books.

Library of Congress Cataloging-in-Publication Data
Vella, Jane Kathryn, 1931-
  On teaching and learning : putting the principles and practices of
dialogue education into action / Jane Vella ; foreword by Joanna Ashworth.
— 1st ed.
      p. cm. — (The Jossey-Bass higher and adult education series)
  Includes bibliographical references and index.
  ISBN 978-0-7879-8699-5 (cloth)
  1. Popular education. 2. Questioning. 3. Teaching—Methodology. 4.
Learning, Psychology of. I. Title.
  LC196.V46 2008
  370—dc22

                                                     2007028786

Printed in the United States of America
FIRST EDITION
HB Printing   10 9 8 7 6 5 4 3

The Jossey-Bass

Higher and Adult Education Series

Contents

To Global Learning Partners
around the world

Foreword

I first met Jane Vella at a Global Learning Partners conference outside of Chapel Hill, North Carolina, at one of the best learning occasions I have ever attended. It was intellectually stimulating, it was fun, the people were friendly, and the showcases and workshops expertly demonstrated creative ways to bring dialogue education into diverse teaching and learning activities. I was invited to sing a song with people I had just met, share my personal definitions of *dialogue*, create a collage, and discuss my values and assumptions about teaching, among other things. In doing all this, I connected emotionally and intellectually with other participants and with the content.

In the midst of this lively international network of skilled dialogue education practitioners there was Jane. Recovering from painful knee surgery, she still held forth with a broad smile, making personal connections with everyone at the conference. I mean everyone. We knew we all mattered to Jane.

Jane Vella lives her life consonant with the values of dialogue education: engagement, reciprocity, friendship, and respect. She walks her talk. Here's one example from her book *Taking Learning to Task* (2001). While preparing to teach a graduate program at a school of public health, Jane wanted to get to know her students personally. So she called each of them up to introduce herself and ask them to dinner. Who does this? Most students were so surprised, so speechless, what else could they do but accept? She wanted to know them and to learn what experiences shaped their lives and to discover what hopes and expectations they had for the program.

Here's another true story. An admirer of Jane's work called her one afternoon, full of excitement, to tell her he had just finished reading *Learning to Listen, Learning to Teach*, and to share how it had revolutionized his approach to information technology training. She invited him to dinner. They sat on Jane's back porch talking into the night.

Dialogue education springs from a place of goodness, integrity, and commitment to equity—values that are also central to democracy. Learners are not treated as objects into whom teachers deposit received wisdom. They are treated as beings worthy of respect, recognized for the knowledge and experience they bring into the learning experience. They are players in the game, not bystanders in an audience. Dialogue education also takes seriously the importance of safety and belonging. It suggests an approach to creating learning spaces where both one's certainties and one's questions are welcomed.

In my role as director of Dialogue Programs at Simon Fraser University's Morris J. Wosk Centre for Dialogue in Vancouver, I live and breathe dialogue. My work at the university involves teaching the theory and practice of dialogue, convening public dialogue, and offering programs that assist public officials, policy makers, community development specialists, meeting facilitators, and educators in learning how to "do" dialogue. Recently, we offered a course on dialogue education to our community of learners in and outside of the university to rave reviews. In small ways and large, the approach reminded me to walk the talk and to consistently involve students—and not to rob them of learning opportunities by teaching at them instead of inviting them to participate.

A question that comes up often from faculty is, How can I bring dialogue into my lectures? How indeed! I was present at a university conference on teaching where Jane Vella delivered the keynote address as an interactive and meaningful experience. We learned about dialogue education by using it and reflecting on our use, by being transformed from a passive audience to an active community of learners.

Dialogue education is about creating a learning space in which learners feel a sense of belonging and inclusion. It is a profound thing to be treated as someone who belongs—with a voice and a right to take part in your own learning—regardless of content or curriculum. It takes a strong belief that the learners you teach have a right to design toward such a relationship.

Taking her inspiration from leaders in adult education such as Paulo Friere and Malcolm Knowles, Jane Vella is a significant contributor in her own right. This book will open you up to a way of knowing and doing that, when taken to heart and moved into practice, will have you understand anew what it can mean to teach and to learn in dialogue.

Joanna Ashworth
Vancouver, British Columbia

Preface

Caminante, no hay camino, se hace camino al andar.

Wayfarer, there is no way, we make the way by
walking.

—*Antonio Machado*

Millennium goals, millennium hopes, millennium celebrations
marked the opening of the twenty-first century. However, as the
first decade of the century moves to a war-weary close, we find
systems of learning and teaching still weighted down by the domination deplored by Paulo Freire in the middle of the twentieth
century. I feel a new urgency to address both the need for dialogue
in teaching and learning and the potential of dialogue education
as it has emerged since Freire's classic work stirred the waters. We
can be inspired and led by his passion for "a world in which it will
be easier to love" (Freire, 1972, p. 6) as we work to replace domination with dialogue in every teaching and learning event.

Freire spoke of the danger of those who "suffered from an
absence of doubt" (Freire, 1972, p. 11). Domination systems cannot
allow doubt. Those who differ are identified as "the evil empire,"
and forces are consolidated to systemically eradicate them. Our
attitude as teachers toward learners affects not only their learning
but also their being in this world. One basic assumption of this
work is the mutuality of education and wider systems: economic,
political, civil, legal, religious. We teach the way we have been
taught until we stop long enough to examine how we are teaching
and decide to do otherwise. Since we live in a connected universe,
each teacher's reflection and awakening affects us all.

I read Paulo Freire's *Pedagogy of the Oppressed* in the nineteen-seventies and recognized then and there the potential of dialogue. The system known as dialogue education has been developing for twenty-five years. I am grateful to Jossey-Bass for this opportunity to present anew the basics of this emerging system, one of whose operative axioms is *pray for doubt*. Although such a system is necessary for continuity and quality control, any system can be dangerous and prone to domination. Walter Wink (1992) speaks of a domination system and *powers* that can take over the best of intentions and ventures. We must be wary of being so sure that dialogue is impossible.

Dialogue education needs that particular axiom: *pray for doubt*. I must doubt this system if I am to serve learners honestly with it. I am called to *fold* the opposites of wary doubt and unswerving dedication into a strong and flexible system that has *learning* as its goal. This is simply good scientific theory. As soon as a new theory and practice (such as dialogue education) has been articulated and "proven," earnest social scientists are moved to disprove, and thus to improve it.

I invite readers to come to this text with that wary doubt, demanding sound theory and empirically proven practice that they can, in turn, disprove and thus improve. No system stands still. With every new teacher and every new context, dialogue education changes, becoming what it can and must be to work in the struggle toward accountable, autonomous learning. Such an aware, scientific stance is deeply demanding. Nothing less is acceptable.

The basic assumption of this system is that teaching is for *learning*. As we distinguish the two here, we will show some high standards for both that can be met as teachers design for learning, not merely for good teaching. Plato pointed out that the end of the Socratic dialogues was indeed *perplexity*. Reaching that end as subtly and serenely as Socrates did involved exquisite teaching. The learning was less exquisite as the perplexed student left in awe at his teacher and somewhat less sure of himself.

When I was preparing *Learning to Listen, Learning to Teach* in 1993, my editor at Jossey-Bass, the inestimable Gale Erlandson, returned my fourth full draft with a note: "Here are some suggestions for revisions to your wonderful book." Her suggestions went to thirty-five pages, single-spaced. I told my sister, Joan, who was working with me to prepare the manuscript: "I do not need this!" Joan wisely responded, "Perhaps there are some people who do."

Gale is an affirming teacher, a tireless learner. She was using the dialogue education approach we were describing in that early book in her management of this feisty old author. And Joan was teaching me through her perceptive challenge, saying essentially, "You cannot give up now."

Notice the human power relations at work here: Gale and I, Joan and I, Gale and Joan laughingly glancing at one another across the country, knowing they had me at "your wonderful book" and "perhaps there are some people who do!" Motivation is being caught in just such an environment of respect, affirmation, and challenge. I learned from Gale and Joan a number of things: I could be motivated, I could rise to the challenge, I had allies in this project (Gale and Joan were two of them), and I had more work to do. These two great women taught me that day much about teaching—and learning.

Recently, David Brightman, Gale's successor at Jossey-Bass, invited me to prepare a book *telling others how to do what you know how to do*. I have taken that as an invitation to offer anew the growing treasures of dialogue education as I know them. The need to enhance teaching skills and learning theory in this twenty-first century is heightened by the global imperative for peaceful systems informed by inclusive dialogue at every level. Dialogue education, as a science and an art, is one way to meet that need. I welcome all readers as fellow *wayfarers, making the way by walking*.

The title of this book *On Teaching and Learning* is a bold challenge to readers to reach into the heart of the education issue and to examine our intention and purpose.

On Teaching

The end of teaching is learning.

Teaching has been the joy of my life. I have been doing it as a professional for over fifty-four years. When I started, in 1953, I was filled with theories and self-confidence. In an unruly third grade classroom near Columbia University in New York City, those theories and that self-confidence began to diminish. As the noise level rose, I admonished the energetic boys and girls: "Wouldn't it be better if you spoke quietly to one another? Can't you get your work done better if you do so quietly?" Finally, eight-year-old Louie stood up in his seat and explained to his classmates: "She means *shut up!*"

That was my *first* day of practice teaching.

My professors in Teachers' College had shown me how to organize a lesson, how to structure a lesson plan and build a curriculum. They hadn't told me about Louie, and all the diverse Louies who have followed me through the years, translating, cajoling, urging, directing me to move from fear into the true confidence of dialogue.

Paulo Freire, Revolutionary Teacher

Dialogue education, as described in this book, was inspired by the work of a kindly, fatherly Brazilian teacher whose roots in poverty in Recife, Brazil, led him to design teaching that could lead to a "world in which it is easier to love" (Freire, 1972, p. 6). I sat at the feet of Paulo Freire in Tanzania, in France, and in the United States. His vision has inspired hundreds of thousands of teachers around the world to use a dialogic approach to teaching in order to confront the ubiquitous threat of the domination system in education, in public policy, in health care, and, indeed, in all aspects of culture and society. With Freire, I hold that as we teach, so do we live.

The day Freire died, May 2, 1997, I was starting to teach an advanced learning course in dialogue education in North Carolina with twelve men and women who had been using this approach for a few years. They had brought to the course the textbook of their own dialogue education designs for scrutiny and development.

We gently celebrated the life and work of this good man before we began our first day of work together. One woman from Nicaragua told of a sacred custom there: when someone thought of a fallen comrade, they said respectfully: "*Fernando vive* (Fernando lives)." Throughout that course, at moments of learning or questioning or conflict, someone or another would say quietly: "*Paulo vive.*"

Freire received the UNESCO Prize for Education for Peace in 1986. Dialogue education, a critical pedagogy, is not an end in itself; it is toward making society what it can be: a place of peace. This means that the classroom is a place of peace; a place of dialogue, not domination. Teaching with dialogue education involves listening to learners at every level, respecting them as subjects or decision makers of their own learning, and evoking their innate power. We design and do dialogue education to prove that such a society is possible and to bring it into being.

Teaching, as Freire wrote of it, was evocative, inviting adult learners to consider their own lives and experience and the potential they dreamed of. He was relentless in demanding quality reading, quality questioning, quality research and study. In Africa he told me: "You must search out all the proverbs, all the tales and myths."

He told a large group of University of Dar es Salaam students that he was proud of one thing he did in his life: "I married my Elza." He knew the generative theme of these young men and women and made a direct connection to them through the fog of language, geography, and culture. The wisdom of honoring generative themes—those ideas that generate energy among a group of learners—is part of Freire's heritage.

One evening, after dinner at our tiny Dar es Salaam cottage, he told us wistfully, "My friends are killing me, with praise." Freire planted in me the seed of the axiom *Pray for doubt*. Freire Institutes at the University of California, in South Africa, and in Brazil carry on this work, as I trust this book does. *Paulo vive.*

Instructional Technology

What I learned in Teachers' College in the fifties was a paper form of instructional technology: how to design classes and lesson plans and deliver courses with efficiency and skill. I learned that well, and I am still studying both the paper and electronic forms. Gagne, Mager, Bloom, and Lewin are teachers whose work is now classic; dialogue education assumes teachers have read these classics and absorbed the basics of design, feedback, and evaluation.

Dialogue education gives a unique, idiosyncratic shape to teaching, without neglecting any of the basic skills. In *Experience and Education* John Dewey reminds us: "The way out of scholastic systems that made the past an *end* in itself is to make acquaintance with the past as a *means* of understanding the present" (1963, p. 78).

Teaching skills involve first of all a philosophy of education, a clear personal sense of why this process is designed the way it is. The instructional technology offered in courses on dialogue education are toward respect and realization of the adult learners' unique culture and experience. Whether in a hospital setting, an industrial training room, or a college classroom, the adult learner comes with a full bag of knowledge and life. Teaching via dialogue means getting in touch with everything in that bag that can make new content meaningful, immediate, and memorable.

Teaching adults for transformation involves first meeting those adults, learning from them about their present contexts, and shaping content so it is comprehensible and nourishing. It is not to distort the past, or the research, or the textbook. It is to prepare that content in such a way as to connect it to these lives.

In the twenty-first century, content is as accessible to learners as the Enter key on their computer keyboard. Teaching that content is more than presenting it in a Microsoft PowerPoint or projected format; it is organizing sets of content in a reasonable and well-sequenced manner, shaping it into learning tasks that are accessible and challenging to adult learners so that their experience of learning is meaningful to them. The examples offered in chapters Eleven through Fifteen show that teaching using the principles and practices of dialogue education involves intense and extensive research and selection and preparation of content.

The instructional technology of dialogue education includes the use of all the classic guidebooks, in such an accessible way as to invite sound, honest, integrating dialogue with and among adult learners. The dialogue is not a dialogue between teacher and learner, but among learners, of whom the teacher is one.

Where Is the Teacher?

Freire wrote "Only the student can name the moment of the death of the professor." I suggest that the professor herself can in fact name that moment when she realizes that she too is a student, learning from the adults in the highly structured dialogue she has designed. When adults are deeply engaged in a learning task, huddled around significant learning materials (a map, a graph, a printout from a website, or a computer screen), in profound dialogue toward the completion of the task, it may be hard to find the teacher, but it is not at all difficult to see the teaching that is occurring.

At our Episcopal church, the priest designed a dialogue education program on the Millenium Development Goals. She invited the adult participants to select a single one of the eight goals that spoke most directly to them. Teams of two or three men and women prepared, with help from the priest, content from the Internet and learning tasks for a one-hour session over ten Sunday mornings. The sessions were lively and full of good learning. However, there was no doubt that those who learned the most from any session were those who prepared it. This is a simple example of an attitude toward teaching that honors the adult learner as subject or decision maker of her own learning.

We teach the way we were taught. Freire's experience in a dominated, domesticated society moved him to reflect on the power of education and to decide that he did *not* want to teach the way he was taught. This is a critical step in the evolution of a dialogue educator: the recognition of all of the implications of a dominating, "banking" (Freire, 1972, p. 71) system of teaching.

Once a decision is made to transform teaching into dialogue education, the same axiom holds: "We teach the way we were taught." There can be no valid courses about dialogue education that do not use it. Incongruity invalidates. Learning to use dialogue education in one's particular situation involves the experience of a new way of teaching. Whether this experience can be virtual is at present a very real question and a serious research agenda.

What does a dialogue educator do when she teaches? In a formal setting, such as you will see in the example chapters Eleven through Fifteen, the teacher's first task is to design. She organizes her content and process with the help of the seven design steps, listens to the learners about their context and their expectations of her teaching, prepares learning materials, and prepares herself to teach the complex content, whatever it is.

She sets up the learning environment with a sequence of steps, building safety and setting the learning challenge. She refers constantly to the learning needs and resources assessment so as to make the essential connection between learners' contexts and the new, complex content. She sets learning tasks clearly and leads the sharing that follows the learning, making endless connections to other aspects of the content being taught, illustrating learners' points with her stories and her factual knowledge, moving them on through the elegant sequence of learning tasks toward the promised proficiency and knowledge.

On Learning

Learning is for transformation toward peace.

The purpose or end of dialogue education is learning; the end of learning is personal and social transformation toward peace. Such an assumption demands uncompromising congruence between the means and the end. If our education is violent, it cannot have the named end. The first learners in a dialogue education program are the designers and teachers. If the end is violent, dialogue education is not an appropriate process.

All that we do in dialogue education—all the principles and practices, all the strategies and technical aspects, all the design and materials, all the decisions—are toward learning. I liken this process to what occurs in a young family when the first child is born: from that moment on everything revolves around the child. Everything.

Although the patterns described in this book are tight and structured, they must give way if they block or impede learning. There is no purity here: only a single-minded purpose. Teaching can get in the way of learning. The design of dialogue education, formal or informal, protects learners in their learning from teachers and teaching that could steal the learning opportunity from learners by telling, or "helping." A brilliant teacher may find this discipline demanding, as it challenges him to focus that brilliance on the learning process of this particular group.

Teachers can get distracted by the discovery of a superb set of exercises that teach exactly what they want taught, or by a reading that captures exactly the thought they want shared, or by an expert whose competence will add so much to the debate or the presentation. In dialogue education, we welcome these resources insofar as they serve learning and are somewhat a part of a design. Again, congruence serves. The operative question: How does this intervention serve their learning? I am reminded of the oath that physicians swear to uphold: *First, do no harm.*

Teachers can get swept off their feet by the sound of their own voice sharing their knowledge or skills. The applause of generations of students and peers is not easily turned off. That was a reward for good teaching. We are now focusing on good learning and celebrate the difference. Materials can get in the way of learning. You may have noticed that a learning task is for the learner. Throughout this book, in all the examples offered, there is no word about what the teacher should do. In most textbooks and teaching guides, these words are common: *tell the students . . . show the students . . . explain to them . . .*

Dialogue education materials will focus on the learners in the act of learning. There is time for telling and showing and explaining on the part of the teacher in the *input* section, in which the directives are to the learners: *listen, write, respond, consider, watch this film and suggest a new title . . .* Learners get good lectures in dialogue education designs. They also get clear directions on what they might do to make the content of that lecture their own.

Materials can be challenging and compelling, complex and comprehensive. They simply must serve learning.

Epistemological Concerns

Freire's constant, delightful question was, *What is to know?* We distinguish *Who:* the knowers or subjects; *What:* the knowable or objects; and *How:* the means of knowing.

Epistemology is the branch of philosophy that studies knowledge. It attempts to answer the basic question: What distinguishes true (adequate) knowledge from false (inadequate) knowledge? Practically, this question translates into issues of scientific methodology: How can one develop theories or models that are better than competing theories? It also forms one of the pillars of the new sciences of cognition, which developed from the information processing approach to psychology and from artificial intelligence, as an attempt to develop computer programs that mimic a human's capacity to use knowledge in an intelligent way (see http://pespmc1.vub.ac.be/EPISTEMI.html).

The focus of dialogue education is epistemology: *What is to know?* This is politically motivated, because as dialogue educators we are bound to be inclusive. Such inclusion involves listening to wildly diverse perspectives and considering incomprehensible purposes. Our epistemology not only guides us, but also compels us to include all who come to learn. Knowing the learners' contexts can give us what we need to design and to teach—and to learn—in dialogue with them.

An Ongoing Research Agenda

What is to know? Were I to build a university dedicated to learning, that phrase of Paulo Freire's would be on the coat of arms. We do not yet know the answer. While war and abject poverty are rampant, we educators are compelled to continue this research toward another hope of Freire's: *to build a world in which it is easier to love.*

Jane Vella
Raleigh, North Carolina

Acknowledgments

Marianne Reiff, dialogue educator and friend, was a constant reader throughout the preparation of this manuscript. I could not have completed this book without her help.

I thank David Brightman, editor at Jossey-Bass, for his initial invitation, and I celebrate him and his staff for their kind shepherding of this work to publication.

My thanks go to all my readers, and especially to the Rev. Dr. Joan Vella, my sister, whose encouragement enabled me to complete the task.

The Author

Jane Vella has been teaching since 1953. She is the author of six books published by Jossey-Bass and a contributor to other texts on adult learning and community development. Vella has taught in more than forty-three countries as a Maryknoll Sister, as director of training for Save the Children, USA, as an assistant professor at North Carolina State University's School of Education, and as an adjunct professor of the School of Public Health of the University of North Carolina at Chapel Hill. In 1981 she founded Jubilee Popular Education Center to do research on adult learning and to teach teachers how to teach adults using dialogue. This company became Global Learning Partners, Inc., teaching dialogue education theory and practice around the world. In retirement at her home in Raleigh, North Carolina, Jane Vella writes from her back porch, celebrates global friendships, continues to learn to play the piano, listens to opera, and kayaks on a quiet lake.

jane@globalearning.com
www.globalearning.com

On Teaching and Learning

INTRODUCTION

Who needs a new book on dialogue education? You do—if you are a teacher concerned about learning at every level. You do—if you are a principal exploring how to design and deliver excellence in learning in your school. You do—if you are invited to design undergraduate or graduate courses for on-line learning. You do—if you are tired of banal presentations of facts and figures that dominate learners. You do—if you are heading to Afghanistan or to New Orleans to train health workers for clinical practice and public health education.

I am assuming that most readers of this book are newcomers to dialogue education, which was born on the inspiration of Paulo Freire of Brazil, nourished on the theoretical work of Malcolm Knowles and David Bohm, and is emerging as a flourishing system of adult learning. Six previous Jossey-Bass publications are available. If you wish to get the whole picture, you might begin at the beginning with *Learning to Listen, Learning to Teach* (Vella, 2002).

The aim of this book is to present dialogue education as a system for addressing the issues involved in adult learning. What can emerge for you are both (1) a new understanding of learning and teaching and (2) a grasp of congruent skills that will enable you to begin to use this system.

The twelve principles and practices offered in *Learning to Listen, Learning to Teach* are still operative and surprisingly useful in diverse global educational contexts. As shown in Exhibit 1, these principles and practices are as follows: learning needs and resources assessment; safety; sound relationships; sequence; praxis (action/reflection/action; respect; ideas/feelings/actions; immediacy; clear roles; teamwork); engagement; and accountability. All will be reflected on throughout this text and shown explicitly in examples and applications.

Exhibit 1. Structures of Dialogue Education 2007

1. *Learning needs and resources assessment*
   To discover their present knowledge and skill with the subject, and their needs and hopes for learning.
2. *The seven design steps*
   Who? Why?
   When? Where?
   What? What for?
   How?
3. *Learning tasks (How?)* using active verbs that engage the learner and ensure both individual and group proficiency in knowledge, skills, and attitudes
   a. *Inductive*—work connecting with the life of the learner
   b. *Input*—new content: knowledge, skills, attitudes
   c. *Implementation*—work using the new content
   d. *Integration*—projecting use of the new learning at home
4. *The principles and practices* at every level:
   Learning needs and resources assessment
   Safety
   Sound relationships
   Sequence and reinforcement
   Praxis: action/reflection/action
   Respect
   Ideas/feelings/actions
   Immediacy
   Clear roles
   Teamwork
   Engagement
   Accountability
5. *Evaluation Indicators*
   Learning
   Transfer
   Impact

This text moves from the learning needs and resources assessment to examining the elements in the basic structure of dialogue education (the seven design steps: *Who? Why? When? Where? What? What for? How?*), to showing how dialogue education is *social* (in the use of learning tasks in small groups), *sound* (in the use of the selected principles and practices), and *sure* (in setting evaluation indicators for learning, transfer, and impact). This simple framework is intended to guide you as reader to practice applications in your own context. By contrasting other approaches to presentation or instructional technology, I invite you to decide, as you read, whether the effort involved in designing for dialogue is equal to the enhanced learning produced.

Applications

Examples of applications to on-line learning situations, to particular classroom design challenges, and to educational leadership efforts in school systems, hospitals, and universities will abound throughout the text and as separate chapters in Section Five. Educators who have studied this dialogue education approach are today designing courses for multitudes in a world of virtually infinite access. Although there is definite structure in the approach, the flexibility and diversity of their designs and applications manifest the essence of dialogue education at work. As a wise mathematician, G. Polya, put it: "What is the difference between device and method? A method is a device which you use twice" (Polya, 1945, p. 18). This structure is a method.

On-Line Learning. These questions will be addressed: how is learning and how is teaching different in an on-line situation from that in a classroom or training context? How do the principles and practices of dialogue education—such as sound relationships, engagement, affirmation, respect, and the learner as subject (or decision maker) of her own learning—apply to virtual learning and teaching? What is the new role of the teacher in on-line learning?

A New World of Team Players

There is little doubt that the twenty-first-century world in which we live and work is different from the old one—and rapidly changing. So many of our teaching practices are derived from another world in which individuals learned in order to compete with peers for select jobs. We recognize the need today to learn together to build companies, organizations, government departments, and national programs that must interlink and work together for the precarious common good. Learning is not optional for a team member. You have the fortunes—and often, the lives—of your colleagues in your hands. You do not have the right to be less than learned, skilled, and enthusiastic in your sharing. No matter what you set out to do today, it will be as a part of some kind of team. Therefore, the social aspect of dialogue education is eminent.

How Do They Know They Know?

Dialogue education is designed to be intrinsically accountable, as it demands that evaluation indicators are in the mind of the teacher or designer at the outset as she uses the seven design steps and identifies the *What?* (the content being taught) and *What for?* (the achievement-based objectives [ABOs] that manifest quality learning). Using ABOs in design shows that we expect to see indicators of anticipated outcomes in the performance of all learners.

How do they know they know? They just did it in the learning process.

Overview of the Contents

In Part One, the fact that dialogue education is carefully structured will be examined, and three basic structures—one for design, one for needs assessment, and one for evaluation—will be demonstrated, analyzed, and practiced. In Chapter One we explore why we structure a learning design in dialogue education. Chapter Two examines ways to do an efficient learning needs and resources assessment in both face-to-face and on-line situations. Chapter Three deals in depth with the seven design steps so essential to effective design for teaching and learning. These seven steps provide the basis for the evaluation structure.

Part Two deals with the *social* aspect of dialogue education. Chapter Four examines why and how we set learning tasks for small groups and reviews research on collaborative learning. Chapter Five shows how individual learning is enhanced and ensured through the group process and corroborates the eminent need for developing team players.

Part Three focuses on the elements that make for *sound* and healthy learning and teaching. Chapter Six reexamines all the principles and practices introduced earlier, showing how these have been applied in diverse global contexts. Chapter Seven focuses on open questions that invite dialogue—a dialogue education imperative. In Chapter Eight we look again at the designer's skill with the seven design steps, which can ensure integration of all the elements.

Part Four deals further with evaluation: how dialogue education can be *sure* by showing how to identify appropriate indicators for learning, transfer, and impact in both the design and the process. Chapter Nine focuses on indicators of learning and transfer, and in Chapter Ten examines the potential of impact indicators.

Part Five offers a synthesis. In Chapter Eleven, we show four examples of short dialogue education courses. Chapter Twelve shows what a dialogue education on-line course looks like. In Chapter Thirteen, we describe dialogue education in professional training for school leadership. Chapter Fourteen considers dialogue education in health care settings, and Chapter Fifteen shows applications of dialogue education to college classrooms.

In the back of the book are two appendices. Appendix A offers a glossary of terms currently used in dialogue education, and Appendix B lists some tough verbs for learning tasks.

This book is designed to demonstrate that learning and teaching are all about the uses of power. A teacher can share information with you and prove to you how powerful he is and how weak you are. This can occur face-to-face in a university classroom, in a training session, in a hospital rehabilitation room, in a community college laboratory, or on the World Wide Web. When that relationship of the "powerful" teacher to the "weak" learner is present, whether perceived or imposed, mandated or elected, that is *not* dialogue education—it is the opposite. This work in designing new educational systems is to prevent the appearance or reality of such domination at every level. As Freire put it, "a neutral, uncommitted, apolitical education practice does not exist" (http://www.paulofreireinstitute.org).

One assumption of dialogue education is that every human being comes with power. The powerful vulnerability of a newborn infant can move a city to action, can bring a smile to the dourest old man, and can inspire art for the ages. Power is a given in the human equation. When men or women are not aware of their power, or are forbidden the use of it, their power does not disappear. Their accessibility to that power may be diminished, but the light never goes off. The purpose of dialogue education and the end of all this effort is to turn the power on.

A Word on Language

Throughout this new presentation of the uses of dialogue education, a concern for language is eminent. Language is the ultimate metaphor for all the principles and practices. Our language is a thin veil that manifests the real teacher and her deepest purposes. Our language, as learners, indicates how we feel about ourselves as subjects or decision makers of our own learning.

Welcome to Dialogue

Your reading of this book can lead you to use dialogue education in your teaching and learning. Your responses to this dialogue, even as you are reading it, are warmly welcomed.

jane@globalearning.com

Part One

STRUCTURED

The more structured the task, the more
spontaneous and creative will be the response.

1

WHY STRUCTURE?

Structure is the backbone of dialogue education.

Dialogue education is a state of mind, moving us to listening, respecting, doubting, reflecting, designing, affirming, considering options, and celebrating opposites. At the same time, dialogue education is a structured system that evokes spontaneous and creative responses to the open questions in a learning design. As educators, we structure our teaching to ensure that learners learn. Structure means safety for the learner as well as accountability for the teacher. In these first chapters we will look at two specific structures: the seven design steps and the learning needs and resources assessment (LNRA).

Building backbone takes discipline and toughness. Structure in a learning design is one of the essential things that make learning happen. Without a structured design, you can have brilliant teaching but little learning. When the event is over, we do not want learners to say, "What a great teacher!" but rather, "Look at what we have just achieved. Look at how much we have learned."

The following *F concepts* are some of the uses of the structures of dialogue education:

Framing. Structures ensure quality learning when individual differences are at play in teams. Structures frame the learning so that each person can do each section accountably and the whole team can move forward without leaving any one member behind. *Learning tasks* (Vella, 2001) are central frames for teaching and learning in dialogue education.

Focusing. Structures focus dialogue so that no one member takes the group off onto an unrelated tangent. Part of the structure is timing:

the shorter the time, the higher the energy for learning. When a time frame is not set for a learning task, the focus is lost, energy is dissipated, and the learning of all is weakened. I have discovered that naming the *end time* of a learning task is most useful to learners. I say: "It is now 9:15. We will share your collected research at 9:45." This heightens the focus on the learning task and the specific content.

Freeing. Structure can free learners from fear and indecision. When a learning task is crisply set—"Do such and such with these particular resources and present your collective findings in this manner by four o'clock"—men and women get to work with confidence and a certain élan. When the guidelines are given, the boundaries set, the content clear and accessible, learners learn.

Forming. When structures are consistent and clear, learners get on with the work of learning along with the work of forming their team. They do not need to re-create the structures each time they begin a new process. Patterns of behavior emerge—including patterns for questioning patterns of behavior. Structures help learners form new theories, new groups and teams, a new personal response to unexpected situations. I liken sound structures to a box with three sides: open enough to allow flexibility and even a graceful exit, closed enough to work in and concentrate. The form or structure is a flexible mold for learners to use to shape new theory and new skills.

Frankly setting limits. A sound structure promotes honesty in the learning session. We will not, within two hours, teach the history of Western civilization or the anatomy of the hand. The structure is a frank admission of the limits of time and energy. It is a way to ensure honesty in the learning objectives.

Fusing. The diverse structures of dialogue education fuse all of the elements into meaningful learning. When a design is competent, professional, and well wrought, learners are so busy learning they do not notice these distinct elements. The structures (seven design steps, learning needs and resources assessment, learning tasks) are often invisible to learners, who are excited about their own achievements and the integrating "aha!" moments of learning they are experiencing.

Graduate students at the School of Public Health at the University of North Carolina at Chapel Hill, where for years I taught Health Education Strategies (dialogue education), often showed me their clinical practice designs with great pride, and they talked glowingly about the engagement and interest of patients whom they taught and of the indicators of learning they perceived. They rarely said: "Nice design for our graduate course!" or "Good learning needs and resources assessment!" Our purpose was learning, and that learning was happening. Teaching and learning fused as graduate students brought in from their clinical internships new theories and new practices appropriate to their contexts. Such creativity is an *indicator* not only of learning but also of the transfer of such learning to life. In Part Four, chapters Nine and Ten, we'll examine an evaluation structure that explains and demonstrates further the usefulness of these indicators.

Functional for learning. Structure is *not* a technique for organizing teaching materials so that a topic can be more efficiently covered. We often hear professors or teachers or trainers say, "This is what I will cover today." However, covering a topic is not what education is about, at any level. Structure is for learning, not merely for teaching. If the structure is not accessible to the learners, or if it obfuscates the content, or if it contains masses of data and information that the teacher hopes to pass on to learners, it is not the structure of dialogue education.

Frequently forgotten. These arguments for structure can be reinforced and corroborated by considering what a learning event looks like when structure is forgotten. A learned professor stands behind a lectern and offers brilliant insights on a subject dear to his heart; he reads from selected presentation slides that colorfully illustrate his topic. Or, conversely, a college class begins with the question, "Now, what do you want to talk about today?" Or a passionate preacher goes on and on, inspired by a line of scripture. Or an art connoisseur weaves through a museum, talking animatedly about his favorite paintings. Or a manager leads a strategic planning session with his staff by talking through all the steps in the process himself. Or a training specialist, demonstrating a new computer program, speedily clicks through steps. You can recall for yourself your own personal experience of structureless teaching that frustrated you and that failed to lead to useful learning.

Structuring Content and Process

When a history professor sets out to teach a university course on East Africa in the twentieth century, she has to organize (structure) the content, of course. She will lay out a set of relevant readings and exercises in a sequence to develop the students' grasp of that content.

A health care professional—an R.N. with a graduate degree in nutrition—designs a community program for seniors on the subject of nutrition that aims at weight loss and weight control. She organizes (structures) the content and prepares a set of presentation slides to show in sequence.

A trainer whose mandate includes professional development courses for principals and administrators in a county school system is invited to design the annual principals' retreat, teaching all the latest legislation related to K–12 education, the issues raised on management in Jim Collins's book *Good to Great,* and a new computer program that all principals have to master. He organizes (structures) these three sets of content and decides to teach parts of each set every day for the four days of the retreat. He too prepares presentation slides for each of the three sets.

In contrast, the preparation of a dialogue education design involves structuring not only the content but also the entire process of teaching and learning. In the history professor's case, she will contact the students who are going to take the course and do with them an LNRA, discovering what they already know about East Africa, what they hope to learn, and what they need to know. She will use the seven design steps (see Chapter Three) to consider in depth who these students are, why their study of East Africa is occurring now, what kind of time frame is available, and where the course is being taught. She will lay out the content in sequence, chronological or otherwise, and identify for each piece of content an *achievement-based objective* (ABO), designing what the university students will *do* with that content in order to master it. Then she will design a set of learning tasks for each of the class sessions in the course.

As the course continues, she and the students will identify indicators of their learning and of both possible and actual transfer of that learning to their other studies and to their lives. They may note indicators of the impact of this course on East African history on them and on current history as it is occurring.

The nurse-nutritionist in the health care setting who aims to teach seniors using dialogue education will meet all of these seniors at the senior center prior to designing her class to do an LNRA. She will design her classes using the seven design steps, laying out clearly who these seniors are and why they need to consider their nutrition patterns. She will select a site that works for the learners and for herself and a time frame that is appropriate for busy retired men and women. The time frame dictates how much content she can select. She will prepare that content in sequence and for each content piece, indicating an ABO showing what the seniors will do with the content to learn it. Her next step is designing a series of learning tasks for the seniors to do, in small groups or alone, during each session. She and the seniors will mark, as the course continues, the indicators of learning that they notice. They will together name indicators of possible or present transfer into their lives (and kitchens) and possibly cite the impact as it emerges and they see one another losing weight and looking and feeling healthier and more energized.

Because the content and the ABOs directly inform the separate learning tasks, some indicators of learning can appear as each task is completed.

This process of designing for dialogue education is demanding, challenging, time-consuming, and strenuous. You will not do it without recognition of the qualitative leap in learning it affords. As you read this book, you will be invited to do dialogue education in your own context.

The trainer designing the principals' retreat using dialogue education will survey all of the principals attending in order to do a comprehensive LNRA with them. Notice that he is also modeling dialogue education. He will consider their responses to questions about what they already know of the new legislation, of Collins's book *Good to Great*, and of the new computer program as he sets out to design—using the seven design steps—the four-day retreat. He will consider in depth who these principals are and why this time is important to them: what is the situation that demands their being at the retreat? He lays out the time frame for their meetings together and examines or selects the site of those meetings. He lays out three sets of content: legislation, Collins's principles and practices, and the skills involved in using the new computer program. For each of these content areas he names ABOs that show what the principals will do with the content. Then he designs provocative and compelling learning tasks to complete each ABO using PowerPoint, a DVD of Collins lecturing to managers at Harvard Business School, and the actual computer program for them to use. This teacher and his students will be invited to recognize and name indicators of learning, transfer, and even impact, as the retreat comes to a close.

In Chapter Two we will look at one particular structure used in designing accountable dialogue education: the learning needs and resources assessment (LNRA). Before we do that, consider these simple implementation challenges regarding *structure*:

Implementation Challenge 1A: Traditional

Consider a course you have recently taken or designed and led. Name one way in which a more precise structure and the F concepts offered in this chapter—framing, focusing, freeing, forming, frankly setting limits, and fusing—might have enhanced that course. Show how you might have used these F concepts in such a way that the course would have been more functional for learning.

Implementation Challenge 1B: On-Line

The structure of an on-line course is really all that the learner sees. Describe an on-line course you recently took that had a *sound* structure that helped you learn, and then describe one in which a less precise structure led to ambiguity and confusion.

A recent experience with the on-line course *Teaching Principles for Healthcare Professionals* at University of Detroit Mercy was challenging and fruitful largely because of the structure of the course on-line. Sarah Swart, course professor and designer, provided the entire syllabus upfront. Each session was carefully structured for step-by-step action, and each student kept her own logbook according to this rubric: Keep a log for each unit that contains the following information: unit name, time spent reading material, time spent working on assignments, time spent on other course activities, things about the unit that were unclear, things about the unit you found relevant, things about the unit that you found irrelevant.

A framework was provided for individuals to use, if they wished. Each week, two separate hours were structured for direct chat via the Internet with the professor. Such a structure proved functional both for learning and for teaching.

Implementation Challenge 1C: Your Context

Name three reasons why you would want to structure the design and implementation of your unique work in your own context. How could such structure be of service to your evaluation efforts? What devices can you design for yourself to support the use of such structure(s)?

2

LEARNING NEEDS AND
RESOURCES ASSESSMENT

The dialogue begins long before the course does.

The learning needs and resources assessment (LNRA), inviting a precourse response from learners about their experience with the content, is a structure that can be helpful in the design of an effective learning event. How is such an assessment done? *Ask, study, observe*—a simple three-step approach. You can *ask* with a survey, *study* available information about learners, and *observe* them in their own setting.

The response of graduate students to a telephone call at the beginning of a graduate course on Public Health Education at UNC Chapel Hill's School of Public Health is always rewarding. I invite registered students to a potluck supper at my home before the course begins. I introduce myself: "Hello, this is Jane Vella. I am teaching the course on Public Health Education you are signed up for this semester. I want to invite you to a supper party at my home in Raleigh this Friday evening." There is usually a profound silence and then a stunned: "Who is this?"

Apparently my invitation comes as something of a surprise. However, graduate students come, with their husbands or wives or partners, and we have a good time while I observe with awe the wealth of knowledge and experience this group of young people brings to this course. I always come away from those supper parties somewhat intimidated by what I have learned about these students and glad for the opportunity to work with them. We had, one year, a young man from the Amish community who had just come back from two years in Central Africa, a nurse who had spent some time in China, two missionary public health nurses who had narrowly escaped prison in war-torn Guatemala, and a doctor who was the dean of the School of Medicine in Santiago, Chile. That was one year.

This rather unusual, informal format for an LNRA is always fruitful—on many levels. It gives learners the chance to know who their professor is "at home," and it gives the professor the opportunity to know what challenges will be faced in the classroom. A more formal survey adds to this information at the beginning of the course, inviting them to review the course design—which includes all of the seven design steps—and to state what looks most useful to them in that design and what they might add from their context.

The LNRA *informs* a course design—it does not *form* it. That is, learners do not decide what they are to learn. They have a consultative voice, offering suggestions on the final design. The teacher, professor, facilitator, or course designer has the deliberative or decisive voice, making the final decisions on what is to be taught. These decisions are informed by data from the LNRA.

An LNRA in Practice

I was invited by The Next Step, a professional organization of adult educators in the American Baptist Conference, to give the keynote and a workshop at their annual forum. My first request to the coordinator was for the opportunity to send an LNRA e-mail to those who registered for the Forum:

Sample Learning Needs and Resources Assessment
The Next Step Richmond Forum, January 2006
Learning Needs and Resources Assessment
I have studied the Next Step website. Now I want to listen to as many of you as are willing to respond.

1. As you try to use adult learning theory and methods in your teaching, what are the areas of difficulty you face?

2. When you went to the website of Global Learning Partners, Inc. (www.globalearning.com), what did you find most useful?

3. If you have read any of my books (see www.globalearning. com), what are your questions and comments?

4. What was most useful in the last national training forum for you?

Please respond to jane@globalearning.com.

A small number of those who had registered for the forum responded. Their responses offered a valuable picture of the group, who came from diverse situations around the world to the forum for professional development and networking. There were few who knew of dialogue education or my work.

I was able to design a basic introduction to dialogue education that served the whole group. If I had not done the LNRA, I would have assumed from my contact with the convener that more participants were actually using dialogue education in the design and practice of their teaching. I would have expected them to be more familiar with the concepts and language of dialogue education and with my books. I would have failed them by not meeting them where they were.

This is the value of this structure: it deals head-on with our assumptions, verifying or refuting them. We cannot build a viable design on assumptions. We can, however, build an effective design on even a small sample of data from actual learners. I did that, in this case, and one indicator of learning was a planning session for an upcoming session that occurred after my keynote. I overheard the entire group ask the leader: "How will we do an LNRA with the learners before we design this session?"

Infinite Varieties

The emerging system of dialogue education includes a set of strategies for learning needs and resources assessment that has been building over the years. The one you choose must, of course, fit the participants and learners you want to survey. There are limitless ways of asking, studying, and observing:

E-mail surveys. I often use a short e-mail survey since it is the easiest for learners to respond to. *Short* is the operative word here: two questions can often give you the information you need.

Telephone surveys. This can either stand alone or be a follow-up of an e-mail survey. This is of course harder to implement, but often, talking to a participant offers depths of learning on both sides that are not available through e-mail.

Website research. Although most LNRAs are mutual, one-on-one dialogue, the study of participants' organizational or personal websites can offer rich data on their present knowledge and use of dialogue education. This can in turn offer insight into the opportunities for practice, implementation, and integration of what they will learn.

Informal dialogue. At times, precourse surveys are not possible. We can always do an informal survey at the first meal or in the first session of a program. Data from such an LNRA can be put to work on day two. It is as important for learners to be asked as it is for the data to be used.

Feedback. When inviting feedback from an opening session, include a brief LNRA extension: How did today's session begin to fulfill your named hopes for this course? What would you like to see added? As the LNRA informs but does not form the course curriculum, it is an ongoing feature of a program. The LNRA never ends. Learners soon get a sense that they are being heard. I always give credit to a learner whose suggestion moved the program to a change that serves the whole group.

Registration. If you are doing work that requires registration, include the LNRA in the registration materials. In this way, learners begin to trust that their opinions are valued and will be considered. I always include the caveat mentioned earlier: the LNRA informs and does not form the course. This frees participants to speak openly and honestly of their felt needs.

Parties, an introductory dinner or tea. There is nothing like the honesty of a spontaneous exchange over a cup of tea or a glass of wine at an introductory party. What does this celebrate but the potential of dialogue? Just as the graduate students at UNC were stunned into silence at a telephone invitation to a supper party, so participants at any learning event can be moved to dialogue in a comfortable, pleasant setting of camaraderie and warmth. What you hear from each one will serve the learning of all.

I am reminded of Thomas Jefferson's dream of his "academical village." He designed the quadrangle of the campus of the University of Virginia as a site where porticos and quiet clusters of trees and benches provided places for dialogue among students and their teachers (http://www.virginia.edu/academicalvillage/).

A Startling Example

It was the second teaching practice in a five-day *Learning to Listen, Learning to Teach* course in Raleigh, North Carolina. Teams were trying to decide on their second teaching topic. Agnes and Sean were doing their LNRA with the other members of the course, and they were getting responses showing indifference or little interest in the topic (about sports) that they had presented. Sean faced Agnes and challenged her: "This response is not only to the topic, Agnes, it is to you. You can do much more than teach this simple topic on sports. Let's take on something really tough and significant." Agnes was reluctant. However, the response to their LNRA had given her pause. In spite of herself, she agreed to take on a tough assignment: as a researcher with a pharmaceutical company. She and Sean created an LNRA survey for their colleagues asking how many were interested in learning about how pharmaceuticals were made ready for production and sale, and what the folded leaflet of tiny print detailing safe use directives and side-effect warnings really said. The group responded with avid interest. One said, "I dare you to make that leaflet legible and comprehensible!"

Agnes and Sean did just that. Their teaching was one of the best I have ever seen. They used dialogue education to prepare a design and teach (in thirty minutes) how drug projects were initiated, implemented, and prepared for market and how that folded leaflet with the tiny print was designed to meet federal standards. The LNRA in this case proved to have an affective potential, encouraging the design and teaching team to dare new levels of achievement. It did not form their design; it radically informed it.

The LNRA is not a device for putting decision making about course curriculum or content into the hands of learners. Dialogue education involves listening to learners, observing their context, and thereby designing teaching and learning that works for them as well as for the organization. In medical school, all that is in the anatomy textbook must be taught; in business school, the steps in setting up a Microsoft Excel spreadsheet must be learned; in a training institute, the muscle movements for post-surgical orthopedic rehab must be mastered. A medical student, an accounting student, a rehab specialist can have no ambiguity about specific content. The LNRA invites learners to comment on that content, to show how it relates in their perception to their unique context, to ask questions on aspects of the content that are not clear. It begins the dialogue. It initiates the process of constructed knowing as professor and learners together construct the curriculum through their dialogue (Belenky, Clinchy, Goldberger, and Tarule, 1997b).

The LNRA never ends. As a course continues, you—the teacher, professor, or leader—are constantly getting new information about learners' needs, wants, expectations, hopes, and capacity. One can describe the LNRA as a state of mind, a listening stance of a good educator.

Without an LNRA

We have all been victims of courses for which the LNRA was not done and learners discover they are in the wrong course. "I know this already!" "There is nothing for me in all this." At a conference, when a speaker goes on and on about his topic, without reference to its relevance to his listeners or their interest in it, we have seen eyes glaze over and knees bob or feet shuffle.

In community education, when funds are set aside for programs that do not relate to the real life of the men and women and families of the community, we see waste—and growing antagonism between the people and the community development organization. Educational programs are not attended, clinics are empty, and the stereotyping continues: "These people are impossible to help." "If only we had the right students!" And "These outsiders do not understand our life and context!"

In hospital settings, patients are asked after the fact about the quality of their care. But, in one example I know of, no one discovered during a long hospital stay that an elderly patient was alone in the world, without family or friends nearby. No one asked those questions as part of the required physical baseline survey. Doctors and nurses are often too busy to listen to patients talk about anything that is not on the physician's checklist. A doctor who is a skilled specialist told me that because patient education results indicated clearly that 90 percent of patients forgot what was taught in a clinical setting, he has decided that it is not worth his time to try to teach patients anything.

The LNRA is a simple, relatively facile structure of dialogue education that has proven its worth over and over. It quietly begins the dialogue with equity and generous grace.

LNRA in an On-Line Situation

Using an LNRA in an on-line situation is simple: it can be done in three steps. First, the learners see the course program originally set up. You as designer have the e-mail address of all who have registered, and in fact, you have an e-list so you can communicate to each and all. Second, you send this simple e-mail:

This is your learning needs and resources assessment (LNRA), which will tell me, your professor, something about you and your perception of this course. You have read the draft course design. Please respond to these two questions by [month date]. All responses will be posted on the discussion board for all students to see.

1. Which of the learning outcomes seems most useful to you in your present work? Why?

2. What else would you hope we address in this course? Why?

Third, they respond and their responses are posted on an LNRA board. Because the on-line course has a personal profile of each student posted, one can read the responses to the LNRA in the context of each student's work and life. As the professor changes aspects of the course, informed by the LNRA, she can ascribe such changes to their suggestions. She can refer to the LNRA responses at times during the chat room dialogue.

Consider how you personally would respond to such an LNRA survey for an on-line course you are taking. Consider what use your responses and the combined responses of the group would be to your learning. Here are some examples.

LNRA for the university history course. (*Asking*) The professor sends a survey e-mail to all who register for the course, asking them to respond, before the course begins, to these questions:

What films have you seen about East Africa?
What books have you read about East Africa?
When did you travel to East Africa and what did you do there?
Read over the seven design steps (see Chapter Three) for this "History of East Africa in the Twentieth Century" course. Name the sections you most look forward to studying.
Why are you taking this particular course?

LNRA for a community program for seniors on the subject of nutrition. (*Observing*) The R.N. with a graduate degree in nutrition who is teaching the program visits the senior center where the course is being given one day and sits in the dining room during breakfast and lunch. She greets her prospective students and notes both what is on the menu and what they are choosing from that menu. She gives each participant a diary at the beginning of the program, inviting each to write down all that he or she eats for one week, without editing what they write. She gathers these diaries, analyzes the data, and shares the overall picture with the seniors.

LNRA for professional development for school principals and administrators. (*Studying*) The trainer spends time with one administrator who describes the retreat programs for the past five years. He reads annual reports from a sample of the schools in the county and compares data with analogous samples from other states.

He reviews the CVs of all the participants to learn their computer expertise and their management history. He spends time on the telephone with a small sample of principals to learn their general response to new legislation.

His seven design steps for the retreat are informed by all that he learns through the LNRA. The learning needs and *resources* assessment is called that because it is imperative for the teacher not only to know his learners, but also to know what they know about the subject being taught. It is vital to know their experience with the topic so they can become mentors of their learning colleagues and of the teacher himself.

Why Do a Learning Needs and Resources Assessment?

The LNRA, an essential structure in dialogue education, is congruent with the underlying assumption of equity and the hope for dialogue. Doing this work prior to a course (and continuing it during a course) is evidence of the professor's intention to listen, to learn, and to serve the learning of his students. He pursues serious constructed knowing so that they may do the same. Constructed knowing assumes "the knower is an integral part of the known so people involved in this sort of metathinking evaluate, choose and integrate a wide range of procedures and processes they bring to the meaning making process" [Belenkey and others, 1997b, p. 63].

Constructivism is one of the philosophic roots of the theories of dialogue education, and the foundation of this process of learning needs and resources assessment.

Sampling in an LNRA. The preparation of a course or program or retreat is a demanding aspect of the teaching role. Adding the implementation of a comprehensive learning needs and resources assessment increases that challenge to time and energy of the teacher. An informal sampling can serve to shorten the task. You can select a random group of students from a large class for your survey. You can observe and study one aspect of their life and experience. A sample provides a great wealth of information about the group, even if it is relatively heterogeneous.

Because doing an LNRA indicates a state of mind of the teacher that will affect the design of the program, any data on the learners will be useful. Learning and teaching are affected by the listening stance of the teacher before the course begins.

Asking, studying, and observing seem simple actions to shape an essential structure in dialogue education. The examples offered here are somewhat formal. However, as your understanding and your skill in dialogue education grow, your creativity in designing modes of learning needs and resources assessment will develop and surprise you. Each unique context offers a new opportunity to design an LNRA appropriate to that group of learners.

Chapter Three reviews the seven design steps, another essential structure that is informed by the LNRA. There is an intrinsic connection between these two structures. Which comes first? That usually depends on the context. A competent designer of dialogue education often finds herself using both of these essential structures simultaneously, weaving new information into one from the other.

Implementation Challenge 2A: On-Line

Consider how you will do an LNRA for your next on-line course. Select one of the suggested methods that seems most appropriate to you in your context. Sketch a design for the LNRA and describe how you think the data from such an LNRA might enhance your course design and teaching.

Implementation Challenge 2B: Traditional

Consider the next course you will be teaching or educational program you are to lead. Sketch a design of a possible LNRA (ask, study, observe). Make the design as simple as possible. Name ways in which you expect the data you receive might inform your design. Consider how your LNRA can affect both teaching and learning.

3

THE SEVEN DESIGN STEPS

Who? Why? When? Where? What? What for? How?

Dialogue education is structured. This chapter invites readers to see how finely structured it is, and why.

The particular structure of *Who? Why? When? Where? What? What for?* and *How?*—once termed the *seven steps of planning*—has been renamed as the *seven design steps* for greater accuracy and honesty. *Planning* is not what we do in education. The term assumes a control over curriculum and learners that does not exist. We plan—and life constantly intervenes. In education, we design. *Designing* means preparing a flexible structure for inviting and enhancing learning by explicitly naming who is present, what the situation is that calls for this learning, the time frame and the site for the event, the comprehensive content and learning objectives (achievement-based objectives—ABOs), and finally, the learning tasks and necessary materials. This structure contains the evaluation indicators, as we shall see.

The seven design steps result in another structure essential to dialogue education: the learning task. Such a task is congruent with the named purpose, appropriate for the named learners and leaders, and suitable for the identified time and the described place. It teaches the content and achieves the learning objectives. The set of entitled tasks shows the sequence of both content and objectives. Exhibit 2 depicts the seven design steps.

Exhibit 2. The Seven Design Steps

Who?
Participants, leaders—how many?

Why?
The situation calling for the learning event

When?
The time frame

Where?
The site

What?
Content

What For?
Achievement-based objectives:
    Learners will have . . .

How?
Learning tasks and materials

Step One: *Who?* Participants and Leaders—How Many?

In dialogue education the first question to ask when designing an educational program is not *What?* (the content) but *Who?* (participants and leaders). Who are the likely participants in this rehab program, this workshop, this training session, this on-line course? Who will be leading this course? This is the operative question, because the learning of these men and women is the given purpose of any learning design. This question is most useful as the first and operative step because it demands that we fully consider the quality of learning that is possible. How were these participants selected? How can we name prerequisites for selection to a program? How can we discover *how many* participants we will have? These are all questions involving the *Who?* that serve the learning. As we saw in Chapter Two, the learning needs and resources assessment (LNRA) can give us a useful view of the participants, their knowledge, and their expectations.

Worst-case scenario. Think of what happens when the *Who?* question is *not* asked in learning events. When this vital question is not asked, learning tasks and materials can be selected that are inappropriate for the learners, the time set may not work for the group, the content is often not immediate or engaging, and the objectives seem to serve the teacher, not the learners. The primary consideration is the learners—their needs and hopes. It is important to name leaders or teachers of a session, of course. However, the leaders can change without affecting the whole program. Not so the participants.

In any learning event using dialogue education, clarity about the *Who?* is our first professional responsibility. Sometimes we cannot know anything specific about the participants; for example, in a public forum or course. We are still obliged to discern whatever we can and ask such questions as, Who might come? What demographic will they likely represent? Will men and women be attending? Who has come in the past to these events?

Just by asking these questions, you are working toward enhancing the learning possibilities for those who do attend. As using the LNRA indicates a state of mind, so this first design step, focusing on the *Who?* clearly shows that your purpose in designing and teaching is *their* learning.

Step Two: *Why?* The Situation Calling for the Learning Event

The *Who?* and *Why?* questions go together. Getting an honest answer to the *Why?* question (what is the situation that calls for this learning event?) controls your responses to all the design questions that follow. There are many perspectives on this question: the organization, the selected learners, the teachers. In *Learning to Listen, Learning to Teach* (Vella, 1994, 2002) I quoted my professor, Tom Hutchinson, of the School of Education at the University of Massachusetts, Amherst, who taught a needs assessment course. He asked, "Who needs What as defined by Whom?" (p. 57). This question reveals the various perceptions of the situation that calls for an educational event or training program. Your job as designer is to use this design step (*Why?*) to get a plausible and honest response about the situation from decision makers and participants. Who among these can name the situation? Decision makers about educational events are rarely participants, or even the teachers, in these events. It takes some discretion to discover who those decision makers are and how to win their support for an honest response to the simple question, What is the situation that calls for this educational effort?

Why? is not the purpose, it is the *situation*. The seven design steps are in an operative sequence. We ask the *Why?* question before determining the appropriate content and learning objectives (*What?* and *What for?*). Individuals interested in designing effective education must know the situation that demands that the learning take place. Inattention to this step in the design can result in inappropriate or irrelevant content—and frustration for you and the learners.

For example, a group of young adults, new to the Peace Corps, are going to work for two years in Tanzania. They need to know something of Tanzanian history and culture. That's the situation! A Tanzanian graduate student is hired to teach "Tanzanian History and Culture" and, without concern for the *Who?* and the *Why?*, he does what he has learned to do and designs a course for these young Americans that is more appropriate for his own graduate school curriculum. The Peace Corps group is overwhelmed by facts and figures they do not need in this introductory situation. They are young adults, new to the Peace Corps, going to work for two years in Tanzania. They need to know something of Tanzanian history and culture, appropriate for this purpose.

Designers can use this phrase: The named *Who? need . . .* to open the response to the second design step: *Why?* A possible paraphrase for this second design step can be *Why?* do the *Who?* need to learn? Or simply, What's the situation that calls for this learning event?

An example. A division of a leading manufacturing company wanted to do a strategic planning session with their managers from around the world. The vice president of the company had called for a new strategic plan for his division. The consultant hired spoke with that VP before designing the strategic planning workshop. The VP described how proud he was to have international managers and selected members of the board of directors present for this prestigious event.

It was a powerful group of forty-two men and women who set out to learn one another's perspectives in order to design the new strategic plan. They worked very hard indeed. A team of administrative assistants did all-nighters preparing the final documents and materials for presentation to the VP. When it came time for this presentation, that gentleman did not appear, sending his apologies to the group. The consultant realized that she had not asked the hard questions that might have revealed the true situation. That error allowed the VP to set up this hard-working group for disappointment and for what they felt was a failure on their part.

This true story shows how important it is to know the situation before you begin to design the content, the ABOs, the time frame, the site, and the learning tasks. Know the *Why?* to make sure that you have as learners the appropriate *Who.* In the example described, the consultant could have demanded that the VP join in all the learning tasks. Whose strategic plan was it, really?

Which comes first, the *Who?* or the *Why?* The context may determine your response to this question. Exhibit 3 shows the integral relationship of both initial questions.

Exhibit 3. The *Who?* and *Why?* of the Seven Design Steps

Who?
Participants, leaders
> Forty young Americans
> Peace Corps trainees—men and women
> Dr. Sembu of the University of Dar es Salaam, trainer

Why?
The situation
> These young men and women need to prepare for two years of work in education in rural Tanzania

---

Step Three: *When?* The Time Frame

When? (the time frame) is one of the most important steps, because an endemic problem in educational design is "having too much *What?* for the *When?*" Educators consistently try to pack too much content into the time available for the learning event. Our society is clearly a consumer society. We are led to believe that our economic well-being rests on obtaining and having and holding more. However, such an attitude is a fatal flaw in educational design. It is a saving grace to be explicit about a time frame (*When?*) that is appropriate for the named participants and their situation.

The sequence here among the seven design steps is determined by the context. Do we first determine the content and then name an appropriate time frame? Designers and professors are rarely able to decide the time frame of an educational program, because that time frame is often a given. A graduate course is fourteen weeks, a training program is five six-hour days, a rehab session is two hours a day for five days. No matter what the sequence, we must be clear about the time frame, taking it into serious consideration when naming the content (*What?*) that must be learned.

When? is not a general question inviting a general statement; it is a critical inquiry demanding a clear and detailed response. What is the *exact* time frame for this session? For example, "second semester" is not an adequate response. Fourteen weeks, three hours a week, forty-two class hours is a response you, as professor, can work with because then you, as course designer, know the boundaries for your choice of content. If the content is a given—for example, Anatomy 101, all systems of the human body—a wise educational designer requests adequate time for learning, not for teaching.

This is the heart of the matter. A professor might be able to teach the complex and extensive content of Anatomy 101 in much less time than it takes for learners to learn it. The structures of dialogue education are designed to ensure learning within the sessions. For good teaching to become learning, it must include adequate time for the reflection that is needed and for the dialogue that results in constructed knowing (Belenky, Clinchy, Goldberger, and Tarule, 1997b).

What then occurs after the course or program or training? That is called *transfer*—the application of new knowledge, skills, and attitudes to life or work. *Constructed knowing* is an expected result of dialogue education. This is what happens when you struggle to learn something: knowledge, a skill, an attitude or behavior representing an attitude, and you do not rest until that learning fits your context, your life. For example, I am learning a great deal these days about computer technology and its capacity for developing on-line learning situations. That knowledge is constructed knowing when I can confidently use it in my work, in my own design of an on-line course. Belenky, Clinchy, and their colleagues compare constructed knowing to *received knowing*—learning that is by rote or for a test. The authenticity of constructed knowing rings true to teacher and learner alike. Constructed knowing takes time within the session.

Therefore, the operative question and design step *When?* must be answered in careful detail: for example, four and one-half hours, or fourteen weeks of one three-hour class per week for a total of forty-two hours; or one five-day week of a six-hour daily session for a total of thirty hours.

The *When?* Time Frame in an On-Line Course

The wonders of the Internet allow for a learner to work on on-line course materials 24/7 for the given period of the course. However, your interaction as professor, with that learner, must have a reasonable boundary. Explicit course protocols can be set to offer access to the course leader; for example, on Fridays, from 4:00 to 6:00 PM eastern time. Such details of this question enhance the learning opportunities of all. The same can be set up for interlearner activity in a chat room. Although a chat room can be *asynchronous*—that is, open to receive comments 24/7—the actual interaction is often *synchronous*; that is, timed. The use of this structure (the *When?* question) makes that distinction explicit. The time frame for an on-line course would include the total time—twelve weeks from July 1 to September 15—and specific dialogue times: access to the course leader Fridays, from 4:00 to 6:00 PM; managed chat rooms with the course leader present Fridays, from 6:00 to 7:00 PM. *When?* in an on-line course must include both asynchronous and synchronous time frames.

Another useful aspect of the *When?* question for an on-line situation relates to assignments. In the Detroit Mercy on-line course mentioned in Chapter One, the professor sent out a weekly reminder of all that was required for the week, including the deadline for the week's assignment. This is an example of setting timed boundaries that free learners to learn!

Step Four: *Where?* The Site

This is another serious contender for the most important of the seven design steps. Obviously, *where* learning and teaching take place deeply affects the potential of the learning. My first course at one of the universities of the North Carolina system was set in a very large classroom, with high ceilings, illuminated by bright fluorescent bulbs. The course was entitled *Adult Learning: Theory and Practice.* One of the central content pieces of this course was "setting the learning environment." I had to admit to the adult students that I was at a loss to teach in that sterile room. We found a viable, less formal alternative whereby some intimate dialogue was possible and learners could connect to one another and do practice teaching. The experience of that course, for me as professor as well as for the graduate students, was deeply affected by our choice of site.

We cannot always change our site, of course, but we can change it around to meet the needs of dialogue education. We can form small groups by moving student chairs, or we can ask for tables in a classroom or seminar setting. The physical layout of a traditional classroom tends toward teacher-centered education. If we want to emphasize learning, we may have to move the furniture.

Learning Tasks Demand a Learning Site

In Part Two we will examine the importance of the social aspect of dialogue education. Small-group work through learning tasks demands a particular physical environment: tables for four to six learners, space for creative work and for individual study. We can do dialogue education in a typical separate-student-seats classroom, but it is difficult (Vella and Associates, 2004, Chapter One). When we have the opportunity to design or to choose a site, the demands of learning guide us. Note that this is not a *learner-centered* issue, but rather a *learning-centered* one. Our focus in dialogue education is not the learner, but rather the *learning.* Effective learning demands a healthy learning environment. That is why design step four is *Where?*

The *Where?* Question in On-Line Learning

Is the *Where?* question moot as we design an on-line learning course? In some ways it is, because on-line we have a virtual site that distinguishes between asynchronous and synchronous situations and does not seem to need further reference to the learners' environment.

However, one further question around the *Where?* concerns the accessibility of the internet site and all that is on it, and the clarity of instructions to learners about that access. In the first week of an on-line course, learners can discern the kind of design work that took place to prepare the course. If the site is accessible and readily navigated, the learner develops a sense of confidence in the professor and in her own ability to succeed in the course. A few test drives of the website of an on-line course can uncover areas where learners could get lost.

Exhibit 4 shows the correlation between the *When?* and *Where?* design steps.

Exhibit 4. The *When?* and *Where?* of the Seven Design Steps

When?
The time frame
> Three weeks 5 days a week, 15 days
> Five hours a day in class: 75 hours
> Two hours a week of field work: 6 hours
> Total: 81 hours

Where?
The site
> Musoma Language School
> Classroom
> Nearby villages, local school, and clinic

Steps Five and Six: *What?* and *What For?* The Content and Objectives

These two design steps go together. In dialogue education, the content (*What?*) is named explicitly and a correlative ABO (*What for?*) is immediately named to show what the learners will *do* to effectively learn that content. The content (*What?*) is named as a noun: for example, major events in the history of Tanzania in the twentieth century; the ABO is phrased in the future perfect tense of an tough action verb with a time frame: "By the end of this session, all will have *examined* and *analyzed* a time line of events in Tanzania in the twentieth century." Note the tough verbs; by *tough*, I mean specific and productive verbs (Vella, 2001). Exhibit 5 displays an example of the design for a *single* session on Tanzania in terms of a particular content and the linked objectives.

In dialogue education we name the content and then design an ABO for each content piece. What would happen if we did not have the *What for?* step, but moved from the content to the learning task? We might then structure the teaching, but not the learning. In an examination of the seventh design step (*How?*) we will see how each ABO can develop into a number of learning tasks. This structure ensures seamless accountability, as learners work through each and every content piece—whether cognitive, affective, or psychomotor—in sequence and with reinforcement. ABOs are designed not to improve on other formats, but to ensure that the sequence moves from content to ABOs to learning tasks. *What for?* is an awkward semantic formulation of a vital step. It might well be called *what learners will have done with the content in order to learn it.* One young man studying this practical theory in Vermont suggested we call this step the "Will haves." The future perfect tense is intentionally used in laying out these objectives to show that it is a learning contract. This *What?* and *What for?* structure of the seven design steps is used to delineate what will be taught

---

Exhibit 5. The *What?* and *What For?* of the Seven Design Steps

What?

Content:

    Six basic Swahili phrases

    Tanzanian history

    Basic practices of Tanzanian culture

What For?

Achievement-based objectives (ABOs):

By the end of these three weeks, all will have

    Mastered six Swahili phrases, oral and aural

    Named critical events from a timeline of Tanzanian history

    Researched Tanzanian history on the Internet

    Read three novels set in Tanzania; identified at least three
        others

    African Voices, African Lives by P. Caplan, 1997

    *Mr Myombekere and His Wife Bugonoka, Their Son Ntulanalwo
        and Daughter Bulihwali* by Aniceti Kitereza

    Village in Uhuru by Gabriel Ruhumbika, 1969

    Identified twenty simple Tanzanian customs

---

in the course and, in fact, how it will be taught—through the ABOs and the learning tasks.

Outcomes or Achievement-Based Objectives

A current strategy in educational construction and curriculum design is to set *outcomes* that can be expected as a function of the teaching. We now examine the difference between outcomes from a course in adult learning entitled *Teaching Principles for Healthcare Professionals* and the ABOs for that course.

Outcomes

Outcomes are usually described as follows:

By the end of this twelve-week course, all participants will be able to

- Describe the concepts of the constructivist theory of education to teaching adults
- Consider teaching from the perspective of other teachers and faculty
- Discuss the influence of quantum thinking and learning on teaching adults
- Recognize their own learning style and apply all learning style needs to instructional design
- Analyze the role of interactivity for both classroom-based instruction and on-line instruction
- Apply learning objects to teaching design
- Analyze evidence-based resources for lecture development
- Identify the different needs for teaching on-line versus teaching in the classroom
- Recognize nontest methods of evaluation
- Develop good practices for instructional technology for digital resources
- Evaluate websites for reliability
- Develop an e-portfolio website for use in teaching material and credentials
- Demonstrate the role of cultural diversity in teaching

Achievement-Based Objectives

ABOs are phrased as follows:

By the end of this twelve-week course, all participants will have

- Identified four concepts of the constructivist theory of education
- Named two ways in which such theory works for them in their learning
- Interviewed a teacher and summarized his or her perspectives on teaching
- Defined quantum thinking and quantum learning
- Named three ways in which quantum thinking and learning can affect adult learning
- Identified their own learning style, using the Visual, Aural, Read/Write, Kinesthetic (VARK) process
- Shown how a design for adult learning reflects differing learning styles
- Experienced in this course the usefulness of interactivity
- Identified learning objects and applied these to a teaching design
- Analyzed evidence-based resources for lecture development
- Identified five different needs of students for teaching on-line and five separate needs for teaching in the classroom
- Named five nontest methods of evaluation and utilized one
- Developed good practices for instructional technology for digital resources
- Named two ways to evaluate websites for reliability and used them on five websites
- Developed an e-portfolio website for use in teaching material and credentials
- Identified cultural diversity and shown how it can enhance a learning experience

The differences between outcomes and ABOs are not only linguistic or semantic. Language is operative. Outcomes say what the learner will be able to do (in future). Outcomes can be seen as transfer indicators. ABOs tell what the learner will do in the session to begin to learn the material. Completed ABOs serve as learning indicators. How do we know they know? They just did something with the concepts, skills, and attitudes, and we have a product as a result of their learning task. To be accountable, a teacher needs the language of ABOs, which is tough and clear and specific. Each separate content piece has an ABO to ensure learning.

Learning does not end with the work in the classroom. Each of the named content pieces is infinite in its extension. However, the learning indicated by ABOs is a specific, sound beginning.

In Chapter Four, when we describe and analyze learning tasks—another significant structure—you will see the tight fit that exists between the ABO and the learning task. This fit ensures effective learning. Once you have a suitable ABO for a piece of content, you have your learning task and you can name your learning indicators.

This set of design steps provides a useful checklist for the teacher, who can see what has been achieved (learned) and what still needs to be done. Professor Marianne Reiff put it this way in an e-mail: "A fine design not only holds up to energetic active learning, but also anchors my course so that mid-term adjustments can be made."

Step Seven: *How?* Learning Tasks and Materials

This is the operative step: naming the specific tasks participants will do to learn the content and accomplish the ABOs. The tight fit here? It is designed for accountability.

The learning task is a task for the learner. What, then, does the teacher do? Research the content, prepare the materials, set the task, keep time, shepherd the sharing of their samples, and comment on each. In that sharing some exquisite dialogue can take place: A teacher may say to a student, "That's an interesting choice. Tell us why you see that event as critical. Yes, I see now.

I would not have thought of that. What are your questions of the groups who shared their sample?"

A learning task is an open question put to a small group, with all the resources they need to respond. The open question may be phrased as a command—*Read this handout and circle the words that are new to you*—the openness there is that the learning task invites autonomous selection of words new to the learner. There is not one set answer to the question or to the command. One useful open question to a group of learners who have just received new content is, *What are your questions?*

Learning tasks are not activities. I am adamant about not using the word *activity*; it is overused. Our learning task is not to make students active, but to enable them to learn what is important and meaningful to them. Active learning is a tautology in dialogue education. All significant learning is active, of course. The *How?* is a series of learning tasks in sequence, teaching the *What?* and achieving the *What for?* objectives. Note that the ABO is often more general than the learning tasks, which are discrete, specific actions for learning. There may be many learning tasks to implement one ABO.

Learning Materials

Materials for learning tasks are accessible, open, and substantive. Accessible materials are readable by the group for whom they are prepared, written in language that is not academic or ostentatious. Open learning materials are a catalyst for learning, not for evoking "answers" from the back of the book. The learning task itself will stimulate clarification, study, and analysis so that the content (*What?*) in the materials can be reconstructed by learners for their use in their own context. Substantive learning materials show that the teachers have done their homework. Content in materials for learning tasks is well researched, up-to-date, state-of-the-art, and immediately relevant to the issue being studied. We do not "cover content" or teach a "textbook"—we teach men and women who need this learning to make better lives and to create a world without domination.

An example of materials meeting these criteria might be the timeline of events in twentieth-century Tanzania. This can be developed by working from the rich materials accessible on the Internet.

Timing. Notice that the example of a learning task mentioned the *end time*—when the learning task results would be shared: for example, "at two o'clock." I find that approach more respectful than saying, "We will share in ten minutes." Learning tasks obviously take different amounts of time, depending on the depth of the issue, the length of the content to be worked, and the difficulty of the skill or ideas being dealt with. Stating an end time makes the learners stewards of the time given and does not imply that the learning can be completed "in ten minutes." When teams of learners ask for more time for learning, a wise professor celebrates their motivations and shows how flexible the structure can be.

Dialogue education takes time. It is difficult and demanding to design and lead education in this way. It is easier to simply "tell them what they need to hear." You must decide which approach is best for you and for the learners in your care.

The Seven Design Steps in On-Line Learning

The seven design steps and learning tasks are a means to establish quality control for on-line courses. When the syllabus or program is set out using the seven design steps, one can see the clarity and simplicity in the design. There will be a pattern of work, in small groups and as individuals, and a set of produced materials to testify to learning.

The congruence between the content (*What?*), the ABOs (*What for?*), and the sets of learning tasks and materials (*How?*) gives the on-line student the whole picture. One of the most serious difficulties with and deterrents to on-line study is the initial need to wade through the materials and directives that usually make up a course. The seven design step structure can be one way of simplifying and unifying that rich and varied set of course materials. ABOs and learning tasks implementing the content can create clear and simple guidelines for the on-line learners to get them quickly to work.

For example, in an on-line course on Tanzanian history, the content (*What?*) and ABO (*What for?*) of a session can be posted. The consequent learning task is available for a cohort study group to do either synchronously together or asynchronously by adding their individual notes to a discussion thread prior to a deadline. Their cumulative notes are available for all to see and comment on. The teacher's role is to affirm, to note her own learning, to add her own ideas. Finally, the teacher can post a synthesis statement: *In the light of your responses and research, we see that* . . . She can add a note about the next session, which will be similarly structured.

In on-line work, where resources are virtually infinite, a central point of the process must be to provide clear guidelines for finding on-line resources and for assessing their quality. The number of named resources is controlled by the learning task, which is meant to develop and enhance learning, not to dominate or overwhelm learners.

A Natural Sequence: *What? What For? How?*

It is a common tendency in teaching to move from the *What?* (content) directly to the *How?* (learning tasks). The structure of dialogue education prevents that by using *What for?* ABOs that focus and sequence the learning. Learning tasks result in tangible products (achievements) that in turn can be indicators of learning.

Implementation Challenge 3A: Face-to-Face

You are invited to teach a week-long session in a master's degree program for forty young AmeriCorps volunteers, men and women, who are a part of the Citizen Schools program (www.citizenschools .org.). They are at the very beginning of their M.Ed. program and need to learn some basics about teaching and learning. Using the seven design steps, sketch a preliminary design for the week-long session, which involves thirty hours of work together. Name one *What?* content piece and one corollary *What for?* ABO.

    Who? Forty young men and women

    Why? They are starting an M.Ed. course to prepare them for work in Citizen Schools

    When? Thirty hours in five days

    Where? Graduate classroom

    What?

    What for?

    How? Learning tasks and materials

Implementation Challenge 3B: On-Line Course

Consider any on-line course you have either taken or designed and led. Use the seven design steps described in this chapter to structure that course anew. Name one way you see in which this might be an advantage to you as learner or teacher.

Part Two

SOCIAL

The dialogue in dialogue education is not between
the teacher and the learner but rather among
learners, of whom the teacher is one.

4

THE LEARNING TASK IN
A SMALL GROUP

A learning task is a task for the learner.

A learning task is an open question put to a small group, with all the resources they need to respond. A learning task is not an activity that follows a lecture to ascertain that the lecture was heard and understood. It is the overarching system that can include inductive work: anchoring of learners in their own context in relation to new content; input that presents the new content as what is added to their learning; implementation tasks that invite learners to apply this new content; and integration tasks that project their use of the new content away from the learning site.

As I explain in *Taking Learning to Task* (Vella, 2001), a learning task is largely a way of thinking on the part of the teacher. It is a moment of great revelation when a student of dialogue education says to me: "Aha! I see, a learning task is a task for the learner." Once we begin to think this way, learning equilibrium is established, and we do what comes naturally to invite learners to learn. When I entitled my first Jossey-Bass book *Learning to Listen, Learning to Teach*, I meant that it was the teachers, not the learners, who were meant to listen. A passive group of listeners is not an active group of learners. Learning tasks are designed to ensure that learners are subjects or decision makers in their own learning. The purpose of such active listening in dialogue education is political, not merely epistemological. It is not learning for learning's sake. It is learning for the sake of the transformation of systems and of society.

Learning tasks done in small groups are a microcosm: this is what society can look like. Here are men and women, working to produce their own theory or skills with ample resources, and a dialogue educator who designed and set the learning task standing by. Here is a small community of earnest learners, focused and committed to hear one another out, to collaborate toward the product: a plan, a context-appropriate theory, a tested skill. There is leadership here. However, it is subtle and moves about from one person to another. There is opposition and there are differences of opinion. However, they are explicit and good-humored. This is not a description of a promised land. These are the qualities of a small group engaged in a meaningful, well-set learning task.

Safety in Design

The small group finds safety in the carefully structured design of a learning task. The more structure there is in the learning task, the more creativity and spontaneity there will be in the response of learners. When there is ambiguity in the design of the learning task, the group loses energy and you hear murmurs: "What are we supposed to be doing?" "What was the task?" "Where do you want to go for lunch?"

Here's an example of a single learning task that could be set in many different educational contexts. Note the tough verbs and the tangible products.

Learning Task: Tanzania: Population Centers and Why They Arise

In your table group, examine this demographics map of Tanzania. Note where the population is most dense. Read the accompanying article and circle what is most useful to you. As a small group, select one population center and write on note cards the elements that you decide provoked such density. Post your population center and your analysis on the wall chart by 3:15. Is the task clear?

Again, a learning task is an open question put to a small group, with all the resources they need to respond. The resources here are the demographics map and the internet article on causes of population growth. This particular learning task relates to this *What?* content—geographic and social elements that provoke population density—and this achievement-based *What for?* objective: learners will have named geographic and social elements that lead to population density.

Note the quality of the learning materials: each table has a current map of Tanzania (http://www.citypopulation.de/Tanzania.html) that depicts population densities, lakes, mountains, ports, and political centers such as national and regional capitals. Each learner has a copy of the internet article on population growth factors. The group must work together to produce a chart with their selected center and their named elements. There is no ambiguity about content: *one population center;* nor about the end time of the task: *by 3:15.* There is no ambiguity in the *title of the task,* which could also be the title of the final display of their learning products.

The indicators of learning are the final displays, the competence of small groups making their presentations, and the quality of questions raised in their small-group dialogue. What about the teaching? The teaching is in the preparation, the assiduous research, and the careful design of the learning task and the learning materials, as well as in the relationship between teacher and learners. The teacher comments, affirms, encourages, keeps time, and synthesizes the displays at the end. She does not steal the learning opportunity from learners by telling. Teaching in dialogue education using learning tasks involves research, design, offering new input, setting tasks, celebrating learning products, and synthesizing.

What Happens in the Small Group?

Once the learning task has been set and is clear to all, we see the dynamics at work in a small group: leadership emerges as one says: "Let's get to it. How about looking over the map in sections, two by two: East, Midlands, West? As soon as you have a population center, let us all know."

Subgroups get to work and discover population-dense centers: Dodoma, Mwanza, Dar es Salaam, Arusha, Bukoba, Moshi. Another leader suggests, "Let's put these on cards and again, take two of them in each subgroup and suggest elements that provoke population growth." Someone else says, "Wait, let's read the article now," and he hands out the article for all to read and mark. One member gets a sheet of paper to write elements as they are named: new ports, airports, new industry, new colleges or universities, mining, railroad developments . . . The subgroups get to work, making reference to the chart of elements to which they add as they think of new ones. Soon there are six charts—one for each city. Someone clarifies the task: "We need to choose one. Which one will it be?" The group makes a decision and completes their chart by 3:14, posting it right before their teacher calls time.

Without self-consciousness, learners work to get the job done together. Leadership emerges from different quarters: artists in the group use their skills, managers move the mini-project to completion. In that active dialogue lies the learning. It did not really matter which city they chose. The learning task was an open question. A wise teacher follows this learning task with one that demands further study; for example, further research on the Internet and publication of a small booklet containing all their displays. This is more than reinforcement of learning; it is building a spiral of learning tasks that moves learners more and more deeply into the issue. Each member of the group can name elements that provoke population density. They can respond with alacrity to the teacher's next question: *Where do you see the next big population center emerging, and why?*

What happens in the small group is *learning.* Our job is to design for it, and then to stand by and celebrate as it occurs. This is not an easy role for an industrious teacher who wants to help. "Sit still, keep quiet, pay attention." That is the mantra offered by Robert Sigmon in 1982. He had asked his teacher to help him to pray, and was offered this mantra. When I heard those words, I realized: this is what a teacher does when a learning task is being completed by a small group!

Leaders and Followers

In every small learning group there are introverts and extraverts, thinkers and feelers, people whose preferred learning style is auditory, visual, kinesthetic—in a word, every small group is a microcosm. Frankly, I do not concern myself much with that which I cannot control. I am concerned that the learning task is clear, unambiguous, well-timed, and possible to complete in the given time frame. I want a learning task to have some kind of product that is both documentation of learning, a step to the next learning in the spiral of reinforcement, and a cause of celebration of the process by which folks learned. At times, it is appropriate that the "product" be a verbal statement or a short written paper. It could be a map or a collage of data, as in the example just given. The product is always original—not a reiteration of the facts learned, catechism-style. So the leadership of creativity is evoked—it could be the artist in the group who has emerged as the leader.

Questions Arising

As learners work in small groups, questions arise that they can answer for one another, or that they recognize they cannot answer. One cogent indicator of learning (see Chapter Nine) is the tough question. For example, during the learning task on population density just described, the question may arise, "This is our perception of elements that provoke density. What do other demographics specialists say?" Then you know that these learners are learning. The teacher can respond with one example and with a series of resources for their reference. She can invite small groups to search in the reference books they find on-line or in the library and to find at least one statement on this issue by a current or classic demographics researcher. Thus she creates a new learning task to take the group to another level. However, her first task is to celebrate the question and affirm the questioner: "What a good question, Paul! This will lead us deeper into the whole issue of demographics and reliability of data."

The small group has taken leadership of the curriculum, moving it to where they see they can and will go. The teacher who is ready to follow, who is able to challenge learners not by pouring her knowledge into them but by celebrating their inquiry and sharing with them the resources she used to design the course, is using dialogue education. Remember, the dialogue in dialogue education is not between the teacher and the learners, but among learners, of whom the teacher is one.

Faith in the Small-Group Learning

When a product is shown or a question is asked, we have to have faith that all the members of a small group were involved: introverts, in their own way, extraverts in theirs, artists offering their skills, philosophers theirs. In Chapter Five we will examine the enhancement of individual learning by the small-group process. The freedom and safety in a small group, sharply challenged by a significant and tough learning task, will permit individuals to both pull their weight to their capacity and ask for the clarification and help they need. Competition in a small learning group is innate. Learners think: *I want to show my skills, and I am moved by your energy and enthusiasm to learn more and produce better.* This kind of competition is fully the meaning of the word, whose Latin roots are *asking* (petition) and *with* (com). In completing a well-designed learning task, small-group members are constantly "asking with" one another how they can do more and better. All of this can occur in an on-line situation as well as in traditional face-to-face educational settings.

The Size of a Small Group

Small groups doing learning tasks can be pairs, threes, or four to six people at a table. More than six can lead to someone's feeling excluded. The design of the small group rests with the leader of the session—and with the length of time available for a learning task. Two people can do a task in a short time. As more learners are added to a small group, the time needed to complete a task becomes longer. You must decide how to set up small groups for any session or any learning task within a session. If there are tables in a learning site, people can face one another as they do the hard work of learning. They feel physically protected by the table in front of them.

When People Find Their Voice

When a learning task is well designed, crisply set, and reasonably timed, we can hear "the sound of learning." An indicator of learning occurs when the teacher tries to get the learners back to the large group from their small-group dialogue. Often, they are so engaged that it is difficult to get their attention.

Dealing with Exclusion

Early on in my use of small-group work in community education I saw a vivid example of exclusion. I was teaching a group of women at a community center in Tanzania. A learning task had been set, and a group of women sitting in chairs arranged in a circle, were working together. One woman kept sliding her chair, little by little, outside of the circle. The others were so deeply engrossed in the Swahili dialogue that no one noticed what was happening. I approached the woman, who was heading away from the group, and asked her how I could help. With her hand covering her mouth, she whispered, *"Mimi sisemi Kiswahili* (I do not speak Swahili)." I asked the group to stop for a moment and look around them. One woman immediately saw that their colleague had separated herself from the group and said, in Kikuria, "Oh, Maria, sorry, we can all speak in Kikuria." She knew the source of the problem without being told. She and her friends simply had not noticed. Maria moved into the circle and the learning task went on—in Kikuria. It is exciting when people find their voice; it is painful when they lose it.

Again, the purpose of dialogue education is to include the Marias of this world, on-line or face-to-face. The purpose of design is to diligently oppose any kind of exclusion. Equity is both a principle and a purpose.

Small Groups in Learning Tasks On-Line

When a well-formed learning task is set in an on-line course, there are many ways to consolidate the individual learning in a small group. Parts of the learning task can be done in a chat room, or products of the learning task can be posted to a blackboard for review by the other members of the group. The final product can be collectively designed. Peers correct one another, or lead one another to new depths and new resources.

Co-mentoring On-Line

On-line students using dialogue education might select a co-mentor: one other person with whom they can work independently and more intimately than in a large chat room. They can grow together, urge one another to keep up the pace and celebrate their achievements in their own way. This can easily be done through a self-selection process using the student roster page. The design can include a learning task explicitly for mentor pairs to do together.

Left Brain, Right Brain

Small-group work is essential to dialogue education. In a timely e-mail I received while writing this book, Paul D. Nitz of Malawi offered this insight on the uses of the small group in learning tasks:

> You wrote: "I can't exaggerate how difficult I am finding it to turn abstract, conceptual content into learning tasks. It's possible, but sometimes my brain actually hurts as I try to make it see things in a different way." I can really relate to the painful pleasure of translating a concept into an achievable learning task.
>
> The way you expressed your experience reminds me of the Right Brain / Left Brain way of looking at things. In "Drawing on the Right Side of the Brain," Betty Edwards writes about this very "brain hurt" that you describe. She writes about resisting the Left Brain tendency to "label" things. Related to drawing, if I see a car and label it as "car," I will draw a representation of a car, really a pictograph. But, if I see a thing defined only by itself and its appearance, then I will be flooded with details that only the un-speaking Right Brain can deal with. Then I will be well on the road to seeing shapes, shades, and angles resulting in a far better chance that I will be able to reflect that particular car in my drawing. I need to see the car in a "different way." According to Betty Edwards, the taxing effort this new 'seeing' takes is really an issue between the right and left sides of my brain. Now, this idea of the left side "labeling" vs. the Right side's intuitive ability to make sense of many details seems to me to relate in some ways to the fundamental shift we make when moving from traditional teaching to dialogue education.

Traditional teaching labels a concept. The labeled concept is taught through definition of terms, examples, illustrations, and exercises. The exceptional learner makes good use of this teaching approach by creating his own way of understanding the labeled concept. He reformulates what is taught by carrying on an internal conversation. He intellectually manipulates the material and often relates it to patterns and experiences in his own life. In contrast, the average learner does well if he remembers the supplied label, memorizes some term definitions, and stores it away for practical use should the opportunity or need arise.

Dialogue education asks students doing learning tasks to carry on an external conversation about the lesson's content with classmates and teacher. They verbally or visually manipulate the material and relate it to their way of thinking and often their own experiences. The presentation of the content (input) will include a label, term definitions, examples, and all the best of traditional teaching. However, the truly meaningful and internal "labeling" of the whole lesson is done by the student, as learner.

Nitz's insight shows how the learning task designs that "verbal and visual manipulation" of the content until learning occurs. Learning is always idiosyncratic. Any two people reading this simple book will have differing perceptions and learning.

The learning task completed in a small group invites learners to articulate that perception, defend it, compromise and pare it down if necessary, but always own it as theirs. Without this fundamental step, creativity and moral judgment, which are synthesizing actions, are impossible. Without this fundamental step, your reading of this book can be dangerous because you might do what it says.

The Four Parts of a Learning Task

There is a natural flow in an effective learning task. The four named parts of a learning task—inductive work, input, implementation, and integration—are not a formula but an indication of that flow. Exhibit 6 provides essential definitions of these "four I's"; a more detailed exploration follows.

Inductive (Anchoring)

First, we want to connect the new learning to what learners already know. We have some sense of their current knowledge from the data offered by them in the learning needs and resources assessment. The first part of a learning task is inductive work, anchoring the new content into their context. Inductive work means

Exhibit 6. Four Elements in a Learning Task

A Complete Learning Task in Four Parts

Inductive Work

Inductive work connects the learner to the task by relating the core concepts of the content to the learners' real life, real work. Learners perk up their ears, tune in, and reposition their energy when something relevant is about to happen. Consider the alternative.

Input

New content is presented. "It takes more than experience to create new learning" (Lewin, 1951). Substantial and challenging content is presented in a nonstatic way. What is the skill, knowledge, or attitude to be learned? Verbs are used for input tasks: *describe, examine, listen . . .*

Implementation

Learners are asked to use the new content immediately, right there in the class. They get to touch it and practice it right away. Action in this phase differs from input in that the learner is *using* the new content rather than responding to it or taking it in.

Integration

When real learning happens, it can survive outside the classroom incubator. Integration tasks ask learners to move the content into the world and apply it in some way. These take many forms: projected uses, tests, projects, or an assignment for next class.

going from one's familiar environment to the unknown; contrast this with deductive work, which moves from the unknown, new content and takes it into a familiar environment. In the example with the timeline of Tanzanian history, the first learning task is to name what event was already familiar to learners. I find this first part of a learning task a gentle introduction to complex, tough new content.

Input (Adding)

The second part of a learning task is input: the new content presented to learners via a lecture, a handout, a timeline, a film, a chapter in a book, or a summary in PowerPoint. This input correlates directly to the *What?* content. Note that putting the learners in touch with this new content is not teaching nor is it learning. Learning involves their engagement with that content. This is why a learning task is a task for the learners. Teaching involves much more than handing over information.

Implementation (Applying)

The implementation part of a learning task is absolutely essential. Learners apply the new content, the input. This third part can be quiet individual reflection, it can be small-group work (as shown in the Tanzania population learning task described earlier), it can be a construction of a contextually appropriate theory from the data given, it can be working with a theory to test or prove it in context. Here's where Bloom's taxonomy of verbs can be useful. We select verbs that invite reflection, creation, analyzing, synthesizing: *examine* this map, *mark* the growth areas, *name* two particular towns that seem to be growing, *reconstruct* the map as it might look in ten years (Vella, 2001). These verbs lead off the learning task that is set for either individual or small-group work. As learners share their responses to these implementation learning tasks, we see their mastery of the content develop, and we can note how they adapt that content to fit their life and context.

The teacher's task here is to deepen the learning through provocative, open questions: *Why? What data seems to justify your position? Where will that inference take us?* Note that these are not "fishing" questions that evoke a predetermined response that fits the teacher's own context. The open question is the essence of dialogue education. It has no skin of judgment on the top of it—it froths into a stimulant that moves learners to plumb the depths of their own learning, test the theory, and feel what the new skills will do in their life and context. If there were one aspect of this whole process that I could name as most essential, it is this: ask open questions.

Integration (Taking Away)

Finally, a learning task moves into integration—taking the new content away, into a worksite, or home, or community. At a recent keynote I offered, entitled "Dialogue Education for Managers," the integration task was "Use one principle you just heard about to deal with a real challenge in your shop." This is the projection place, where learners move vicariously into the future and antici-pate how they can use this learning in real life.

Every learning task does not have to have four distinct parts, but a set of tasks will have this general flow—from work that con-nects their context to the new content (anchors it), to a presenta-tion of the new content (adds), to doing something with that new content in a devised situation (applies), to taking the new content home (takes away). This design can help us teachers protect the learning space from our own enthusiasm for telling what we know. The four parts move learners ineluctably toward authentic owner-ship of the content, whether that content is a new set of skills or challenging concepts or behaviors manifesting attitudes.

Note how intensely structured the learning task is. This is not an open system. It is carefully designed for learning the con-tent the teacher intends to teach. The small group is the place of learning, whether on-line or face-to-face. As learners talk and work together, practicing the behaviors they are learning, pro-ducing the manifestation of their learning, struggling to compre-hend and contextualize the new concepts or skills, neither they nor the teacher can immediately evaluate the quality or quantity of that learning. Learning indicators are indeed behaviors (see Chapter Nine); however, these behaviors are a result of learning as well as indicators of it. This intense engagement with significant new content is a sacred time—a moment of emergence of new beings, with new knowledge and skills. Learners of any age stand taller and look with affection on their hard-working colleagues. Having completed meaningful learning tasks together, they know that they know.

Implementation Challenge 4A: Learning Tasks On-Line

If you design on-line courses, take one presentation and transform it into a series of learning tasks, guided by the four I's model: inductive work, input, implementation, and integration. Invite learners to do their work solo, share it with their co-mentor or colleagues on-line, and then synthesize it into their own presentation of the new learning.

Implementation Challenge 4B: In a Traditional Classroom

Take any course you are presently teaching or studying. Select a single chapter or even a single topic. Turn the narrative content into a learning task, using the four I's. Remember the axiom: *Don't tell what you can ask. Don't ask if you know the answer. Tell, in dialogue.*

5

INDIVIDUAL LEARNING ENHANCED

Ultimately, the responsibility for learning is
the individual's. This learning is supported and
nourished by the small group.

Small-group work on learning tasks does not in any way diminish the responsibility of each individual for her own learning, nor
the responsibility of the teacher to design accountable learning
tasks. What happens in the small group is designed to enhance the
individual's learning. Only an individual can change her own
behavior. Transformation occurs one person at a time.

Energy. Small-group work can energize individuals so that they
learn faster and with greater accuracy. Each person's efforts in the
small group will be shaped by her personal style. Whether a strong
extravert or an introvert, she can offer her part to the learning task
in her own way. Some learners add most by quiet listening, with an
occasional word that focuses or intensifies the dialogue. Some learners (I am one of them) must speak to know what they are thinking.
Every small group has the chance of having every type represented. It
is not necessary or even possible to set up groups by type. Synchronicity is an ally in dialogue education. Most groups work well to get
the learning tasks done and to enhance the learning of all involved.

Diversity. Each person's solo learning follows his or her own
predilections and type. In a small group doing learning tasks, each
individual is challenged to look at another side of an issue, to
move into places he or she would prefer to avoid. Carl Jung warns

us against stereotypes, while explaining preferred type. We are all capable of behavior using all of the eight types: introvert, extravert, intuitive, sensing, thinking, feeling, perceiving, judging (Kiersey and Hatch, 1984). The fact that we each have a preferred type is important knowledge; it is neither a boundary nor a tether. Watch an Extravert, Intuitive, Feeling, Perceiving woman as she acts at times from her "inferior" functions: Introvert, Sensing, Thinking, Judging. She can do that well when the occasion calls for it.

Productivity. In learning as in life, many hands often make better work. What a small group can achieve in a given time toward a product manifesting their learning is not only more than what a solo learner can achieve, but also deeper. There are times during a learning task when a small group wisely decides it is time for all members to sit quietly and think, to plan or to read content material again, or to sketch a draft design as individuals and then share them. Once these items are put together, and the energy of the small group is brought to the synthesis, it is evident that a learning task done in a small group can be productive.

Protection. There are both strengths and weaknesses among the learners in a small group doing a learning task. If the task were on statistics, for example, the literary woman might not be a strong member. However, the learning group can protect her weakness by setting up a mentoring system or by just making sure that she keeps up with the tasks at hand. Protection is everyone's job and is in everyone's interest. She, in turn, will be on hand to write the report.

Getting the Job Done. When a learning task is set and the small group goes to work on it, they must be clear that their completion of the job together is *not* the objective of the task. The purpose of the learning task is learning for all. When someone in the group is struggling to learn, it may be that the task is badly set, or that the group has misconstrued or misunderstood it. Clarification is a major role of the teacher. When the teacher sees a group struggling, she can go to them and offer, "How can I make the task clear?" This is not an intrusion; it assumes that the problem is with the phrasing of the learning task, not with the abilities of the learners. Such a clarification can lead to intense activity and focused learning. The "weak" member's honesty in describing her confusion led to a necessary clarification for all members.

Pace. This is an important issue for small-group work. Who sets the pace for the learning task? Again, in any small group, we have people who work at a different pace. Remember, you as teacher set the time frame for the task. Learners work within that framework and can, if need be, extend it on their request. But the framework exists. They must be helped to realize that within a learning task learning takes place, but not *all* the possible learning about a content piece. They can continue this learning after the learning task is completed, and you hope they will. Transfer of learning continues learning. Assignments for further research can guide this later learning. Internet research possibilities on any subject are virtually infinite. When a group is used to dialogue education and learning tasks, members become sensitive to the issue of pace, and they watch one another for signs of distress. Initially, it is the teacher's role to keep an eye on each learning group to catch any self-exclusion. The story of Maria in Chapter Four reflects the rewards of such attention. Groups soon take on that role themselves. They realize that this facet of the protection role works for each of them.

Inclusion. We work on learning tasks in small groups for the purpose of not excluding anyone from the learning. Remember our initial political purpose? Dialogue education is not learner-centered, but *learning*-centered—and that means learning for each and all. Tests and other individual measures are useful in celebrating the extent of each person's learning. However, they are minimal. So much more is learned than we can measure. We will examine this further in Chapter Nine as we look at evaluation. Dialogue education demands that we trust the group to be a safe place for learning for all, without exception. No one is excluded from her own potential.

Phrasing. The language of a learning task can provide clarity and crispness and a sense of the autonomy of the learners. I try to avoid this phrasing: "What *I want you to do* now is . . . ." Such peremptory phrases subtly indicate that you as teacher are the only decision maker, the subject, in this venture. You are not. Read the learning task as set out in your design. You have worked hard to select tough, active verbs; use them. Set the end time: "We will share your research at 3:15." When a question is asked, answer it and stop after the answer. It is a great temptation to tell learners all of your responses and ideas about the learning task and thereby steal the learning opportunity from the learners. In the same vein, because you know the learners can read, avoid reading what is written on a PowerPoint slide.

Input. PowerPoint has great potential as a visual aid for learners. PowerPoint presentations can be the epitome of what Paulo Freire calls "the banking system of education" (Freire, 1972), or they can be a stimulating *input* aspect of a dynamic learning task (Vella, 2001). PowerPoint can also be used as a weapon of mass domination. We all know the drill: a teacher designs a colorful, bright, large-print PowerPoint sequence with brilliant visual effects and clever sayings. In the very design of such a presentation we as teachers can feel *the point of power.* When we face an audience and make our presentation, we demonstrate our command of the content and our skill with the process of presenting information. Our audience leaves, nodding in awe at our visible knowledge and power. We *are* the point of power, having used PowerPoint to demonstrate that. In so doing we can miss the point of learning. The purpose of dialogue education is to invite men and women of all ages to celebrate their own power as they contemplate, examine, struggle with, and manage for their own context new learning, new content. Our assumption is that the learners bring their own "points of power" as they name their unique and idiosyncratic context (inductive work), examine new research and content (input), do something meaningful with that content (implementation) and bring that content home to renew their context (integration). These, again, are the four parts of a dialogue education learning task.

PowerPoint slides can be a brilliant way of presenting the new content (input) in a visual and sequenced mode, with large print and as clever a set of sayings as we wish. However, it is only *one-fourth* of the process. Learning happens when all four parts of the process are afforded time and attention. When we celebrate the learners as points of power, constructing their learning to fit their context, we make the best use of PowerPoint. Here are some examples of the use of PowerPoint to enhance learning tasks.

Example: Scripture Studies

Learning Task 1: Major Themes in the Gospel of Mark

Who: graduate students in a D.Min. course on the Gospel of Mark

Inductive work (anchoring the new learning in the context of the learners):

1A. In pairs, open Mark's gospel and examine it from beginning to end by opening to at least ten random passages. Share what you remember about this gospel from earlier readings. Describe a time when this gospel touched you in some way. Tell what you recall as unique about this Gospel of Mark. We'll hear a sample.

Input (adding knowledge or skills):

1B. Watch this PowerPoint presentation of the main points of *Mark as Story* (Rhoads, Dewey, and Michie, 1999). As your questions arise, write them on your copy of the presentation. We'll hear and respond to all of these questions at the end.

The Gospel of Mark (c. 66–70 C.E.). The author creates a story world, a narrative, to make his point.

Five key features of a narrative:

- Narrator: the voice, point of view, tone of the storyteller
- Setting: the context: the depiction of the cosmos, social world

- Plot: events: their order, sequence, conflicts, development
- Characters: actors in the story, their identity, motives, relations
- Rhetoric: the way the author uses features of the narrative to persuade

Guidelines for Reading Mark as a Story
- Look at this story as a portrayal of Jesus and disciples as they are in the narrative, not as a window into history.
- Read Mark's story independently of the other gospels. It is complete.
- Avoid reading modern cultural assumptions into this first century story.
- Avoid reading modern ideas about Jesus or God into this story.

Source: Adapted from Rhoads, Dewey, and Michie, 1999.

Implementation (Applying the New Data to a Situation):

1C. In table teams of threes, select *one* of the five concepts presented by Rhoads, Dewey, and Michie—the narrator, the setting, the plot, the characters, or the rhetoric—and re-present the argument for reading Mark *as a story* for one of these groups:

A group of high school youth: men and women

A group of senior citizens living in a retirement community

A parish Sunday school class

We'll hear the argument from each table group.

1D. At your table, consider *one* of the guidelines offered. Show an example of using that guideline in reading the Gospel of Mark with any one of these groups. We'll hear all your examples.

A dialogue education use of PowerPoint involves designing a learning task with *inductive* work, *input* via a PowerPoint presentation, and *implementation*—an invitation to learners to do something with the new content. You can set this as three learning tasks or three parts of one learning task. The fourth part, or the fourth task, is a projection task—inviting learners to take this home to their own context and do something there with the input. (*Integration*: take it away!)

The next time you hear a section of Mark's gospel, note how enhanced the lesson is when you think of it in terms of narrator, plot, setting, rhetoric, and characters. Notice how the PowerPoint presentation summarizes but does not supplant the reading of the source text.

The basic epistemological assumption of dialogue education is that learning is not merely a transfer of information; rather, it is a use of new content in learners' real-life context, to renew that context and also to reexamine and refit the data.

Example: Nutrition

Learning Task 2: Nutrition: The Art of Portion Control

Who: Men and women with weight problems

Inductive work (anchoring the new learning in the context of the learners):

2A. In pairs, describe one very effective method you have used to lose weight. Name what you saw as the greatest obstacle to keeping lost weight off. We'll hear a sample.

Input (adding knowledge or skills):

2B. Watch this PowerPoint presentation of some basic facts from recent and current research on one aspect of weight loss: the science of portion control. Write on your copy of the PowerPoint handout what you agree with or disagree with in this research. Circle the ideas you find most useful. We will hear and respond to all you have written.

Research on Weight Loss: Portion Control

Standard Servings. Standard serving sizes, from Nutrition Facts labels, can help you judge how much you are eating. When cooking for yourself, use measuring cups and spoons to measure your usual food portions and compare them to standard serving sizes. Put the measured food on a plate before you start eating.

What About Foods Without a Nutrition Facts Label? For foods that don't have a nutrition facts label, such as ground beef, use a kitchen scale to measure the food in ounces (according to the Food Guide Pyramid, one serving of meat, chicken, turkey, or fish is 2 to 3 ounces).

Ideas to Help You Control Portions at Home

- Take a standard serving out of the package and eat it off a plate instead of eating straight out of a box or bag.
- Avoid eating in front of the TV or while busy with other activities.
- Eat breakfast every day.
- Pay attention to what you are eating and fully enjoy the smell and taste of your foods.
- Eat slowly so your brain can get the message that your stomach is full.
- Take seconds of vegetables or salads instead of meats or desserts.
- Try to eat three sensible meals at regular times throughout the day.
- Skipping meals may lead you to eat larger portions at your next meal.
- When cooking in large batches, freeze food in single-meal-sized containers that you will not serve right away. This way, you won't be tempted to finish eating the whole batch before the food goes bad. And you'll have ready-made food for another day.

- Keep snacking to a minimum.
- When you do have a "treat," eat only one serving, eat it slowly, and enjoy it!

Control Portions When Eating Out. Try to prepare more meals at home. Eat out and get take-out foods less often. When you do eat away from home, try these tips to help you control portions:

- Share your meal, order a half-portion, or order an appetizer as a main meal.
- Stop eating when you begin to feel full. Focus on enjoying the setting and your friends or family for the rest of the meal.
- Avoid large beverages. Order the small size, choose a calorie-free beverage, or drink water with a slice of lemon.
- If you stop at a fast food restaurant, choose one that serves salads, or order the small burger with lettuce and tomato.

Source: Adapted from NIH Publication No. 03–5287, Just Enough For You: About Food Portions.

Implementation (Applying this New Data to our Context):

2C. In the same original pairs, consider what you named your most effective method for losing weight. Explain how *portion control*, as described in the PowerPoint presentation, can enhance what you already know. We'll hear a sample. Consider again the obstacles you named to keeping weight off. Tell how this science of portion control might serve you in dealing with those particular obstacles. We'll hear a sample.

Integration: Take it away!

2D. *Design* one practical tool you personally can use to document your efforts at the science of portion control. We'll see all of these tools.

Notice, in these two simple examples about *the point of power*, that all learners are engaged in constructing meaning of the new content. Their context is respected as a valid matrix for the development and reconstruction of this content. They are recognized as the subjects of the process: what they decide to do with the content is valid until proven invalid. Teaching involves designing a careful sequence of the content in the PowerPoint presentation; the fourfold learning task honors the cognitive, affective, and psychomotor aspects of learning. Small-group work enhances the possibility of successful learning, using open questions both in the small-group setting and in the sharing in the larger group. Remember the axiom: *Don't tell what you can ask; don't ask if you know the answer; tell in dialogue.*

Power is of course, everywhere: sunlight, water, human energy. The danger occurs when the professor (or priest, or parent, or manager) claims power as his alone and names one singular point of power as he reads aloud the PowerPoint presentation.

Learners often speak of the *magic* they experience in good learning. I propose the magic lies in the recognition and use of the multiple points of power in the room. When a PowerPoint presentation is one part of a session, evoking the other points of power to examine it, to critique it and to use it for their own context, the magic of learning unfolds.

Individual Learning Enhanced On-Line. The individual learner in an on-line course can feel very much alone and isolated. A great deal of initial design work has to occur to make sure learners feel welcomed and vital to the learning of all. The published roster with profiles, the shared LNRA responses, a mentoring system, an initial invitational task—all can enhance individual learning. The more learners can offer in the LNRA about themselves and their interests, their fears and their present knowledge, the more they will feel a part of this learning enterprise.

Without such attention, an individual learner may do all the work and still never be incorporated into the dialogue. In a recent design session, a friend, after a long day of hard work to create just the right design for her project, said, "Aha! Now I know why people do not use dialogue education! It is too hard and takes too much time to prepare."

My response was heartfelt: "Of course it is hard, and it does take time to do thorough preparation. Quality learning demands quality work from quality teachers."

A continuing feedback mechanism in an on-line course is one way to maintain inclusion and engagement. "How are you doing? How was this session different from others? How would you measure your learning in this unit?" Such open questions invite a dialogue on feedback. Mentoring teams in an on-line course can offer one another such attention, feedback, and support. So often a small clarification can make an on-line task possible and immediately useful to a learner. However, learners must recognize that they must own their confusion, name it, and ask for clarification. When they are affirmed in such a request and the clarifying amendment is celebrated, they will be quicker to ask the next question. Learning on-line is such a complex new science that we need to document and celebrate any and all tactics and strategies that work for learners. (See Chapter Twelve for an example of a dialogue education on-line course.)

Implementation Challenge 5A: Face-to-Face

In an urban setting, you are teaching a group of prenatal women "Nutrition for Pregnancy," with emphasis on their need for folic acid. The content about folic acid has been researched from the Internet. Review the following learning tasks; what changes will you make to fit an urban audience of pregnant women?

Learning Task 1 (Inductive Work)
Listen to this story of Anna. In pairs, tell how you relate to it from your own history of pregnancy.

"I took a separate folic acid supplement after I found out I was pregnant with my first child. I tried to get pregnant with him for two years. The next time I decided to try to get pregnant I started taking folic acid right away. I had been taking it for one month when I got pregnant on the first try with baby #2." Anna

Learning Task 2 (Input): Folic Acid and Pregnancy

Listen to this reading from the handout on folic acid; circle what you find useful and write out your questions. We'll hear all that you circled, and respond to your questions.

Folic Acid and Pregnancy

For a healthy baby, get enough folic acid every day—especially before conception and during early pregnancy.

What is Folic Acid?

Folic acid, sometimes called folate, is a B vitamin (B9) found mostly in leafy green vegetables like kale and spinach, orange juice, and enriched grains. Repeated studies have shown that women who get 400 micrograms (0.4 milligrams) daily prior to conception and during early pregnancy reduce the risk that their baby will be born with a serious neural tube defect (a birth defect involving incomplete development of the brain and spinal cord) by up to 70%.

The most common neural tube defects are spina bifida (an incomplete closure of the spinal cord and spinal column), anencephaly (severe underdevelopment of the brain), and encephalocele (when brain tissue protrudes out to the skin from an abnormal opening in the skull). All of these defects occur during the first twenty-eight days of pregnancy—usually *before* a woman even knows she's pregnant.

That's why it's so important for all women of childbearing age to get enough folic acid—not just those who are planning to become pregnant. Any woman who could become pregnant should make sure she's getting enough folic acid.

Doctors and scientists know that this vitamin is crucial in the development of DNA. As a result, folic acid plays a large role in cell growth and development, as well as tissue formation.

Getting Enough Folic Acid

The U.S. Centers for Disease Control and Prevention (CDC) recommends that all women of childbearing age—and especially those who are planning a pregnancy—consume about 400 micrograms (0.4 milligrams) of folic acid every day. Adequate folic acid intake is very important *one month before conception and at least three months afterward* to potentially reduce the risk of having a fetus with a neural tube defect.

In 1998, the Food and Drug Administration mandated that folic acid be added to enriched grain products. You can boost your intake by looking for breakfast cereals, breads, pastas, and rice containing 100% of the recommended daily **folic acid allowance**. But for most women, eating fortified foods isn't enough. To reach the recommended daily level, you'll probably need a vitamin supplement. Some health care providers even recommend taking a folic acid supplement in addition to your regular prenatal vitamin. *Source:* Adapted from KidsHealth for Parents, n.d.

Learning Task 3 (Implementation)

Design a weekly food and supplement diet for yourself or a friend who is trying to get pregnant. Circle the items in that diet that are rich in folic acid. Sign your weekly food program and post it. We'll examine all.

Learning Task 4 (Integration)

Barbara has recently married and hopes to soon be pregnant. Barbara knows nothing about folic acid or nutrition for pregnancy. She writes you, her friend, about how anxious she is to have a baby soon. Write a letter to Barbara telling her what you have learned about the importance of folic acid in pregnancy. Send that letter to your teacher. We'll share your letters at our next class.

Implementation Challenge 5B: On-Line

You are setting up an college credit on-line course in economics for undergraduate students. You have a chat room for an hour of synchronous dialogue with the students each Friday and a mutual mentoring system. It is week three; the content is difficult for many of the learners. One student writes you an e-mail indicating that her mentor has told her to simply read the chapter again. She is still confused about the content in the chapter.

Name one way you might address this individual learner's need, using what you have read in this chapter on Individual Learning. Name a few things you would *not* do and tell why.

Part Three

SOUND

These principles and practices make a
difference in design and in teaching.

6

PRINCIPLES AND PRACTICES

Current State of the Art

A principle is the beginning of action.

In 1994, *Learning to Listen, Learning to Teach: The Power of Dialogue in Educating Adults* was published. It featured a set of twelve basic principles and practices for effective adult learning. These have influenced adult educators around the world, who have discovered that their work is to adjust these principles and practices to work in their unique context. Engagement in Kabul, Afghanistan, is not the same as engagement in Kansas City, Missouri. But it is engagement. Sound learning involves these basic principles and practices—and many more still to be discovered.

The original twelve principles were learning needs and resources assessment; safety; sound relationships; sequence and reinforcement; praxis (action/reflection/action); respect; ideas/feelings/actions; immediacy; clear roles; teamwork; engagement; and accountability. They still work to make an educational design sound for learning. In 2007 there are new critical connotations for each of these principles and practices, especially as we consider them working for us in an on-line context. The overall principle is dialogue that works toward learning in any context.

Needs Assessment

The dialogue begins before the learning event. Essential to dialogue education has been the practice of doing a learning needs and resources assessment (LNRA) prior to any educational event.

We have looked intently at this practice in Chapter Two. You will recall that the LNRA begins the dialogue long before the event occurs, and that data from that survey informs—but does not form—the design for learning.

This simple tool (ask, observe, study) gives a perspective on the expectations of learners, their competencies in the field, and their hopes and fears about the event. It is always surprising to hear from learners who are usually shocked that anyone asked about their hopes for a course and about their present competency. It takes very little to invite learners to define their learning needs and present resources.

Here is another example of an LNRA. Today, as I set out to design a workshop for professors at a university in western Canada, I sent the coordinator this e-mail LNRA survey to share with a group of participants:

Learning Needs and Resources Assessment

Annual Symposium on Innovative Teaching

"Dialogue in Teaching and Learning: An Educational Framework for Linking Coursework and Community." This three-day symposium will explore the challenges and rewards associated with dialogue-based learning as an innovative practice in pedagogy. Please respond to these two questions about your expectations and hopes for the keynote and workshop.

1. How do you use dialogue education in your teaching?

2. What are your concerns and questions about the use of dialogue education in your context?

Note that the survey comes from the coordinator of the symposium, with her authority to invite responses from whomever she chooses. A sample of those registered will give enough data. I write an e-mail to each participant who responds—reinforcing the dialogue. The survey is one form of the LNRA; I also study the website of the university and of the particular department or program. I read on the Web about the surrounding towns and the history of that part of the country. In short, I prepare myself as designer and teacher for a cross-cultural experience. That would be necessary whether I was planning to travel one hundred and fifty miles down Route 85 to a university in Charlotte, N.C., or three thousand miles to one in Canada.

The program of the particular event is another source of information, and a long conversation with the event coordinator is also a part of the LNRA. Once you get moving on this needs assessment research, you will be surprised how many different routes open up to you. Again, all that is needed on our part as we do needs assessment is a disposition to listening and learning. The process, the particular tools, the arrangement of the data is up to you. What is not an option, if you want to design effective learning, is omitting it.

Needs Assessment in an On-Line Situation

The great advantage of an on-line situation is that needs assessment can go on continually. In an accruing dialogue, there is always the possibility for a learner to reframe her needs and expectations, to indicate that she wants to go further or not as far as originally declared. In any learning-centered course, the needs assessment is continuous; it is just more possible and explicit on-line.

As on-line students grow to know one another and each other's backgrounds over time, they discover one another to be unexpected resources. Initially, some intimidation is at play as a course shapes itself. A learner may not think of making explicit a particular skill or experience that is invaluable to the learning cohort. With a disposition to listening and learning, the professor or teacher opens those resources to the group. The learning needs and resources assessment never ends.

Safety in Learning

I have learned how important it is to "hold the opposites" as you use design principles in a particular context. Most adults come to an adult learning event to be challenged. They want the envelope to be pushed, their minds to be stretched, and their creativity whetted. However, none of that can occur without the principle of safety at work.

Safety is created by starting the dialogue long before you start the course or the learning event. Safety is ensured not through words but through the behavior of the teachers. Learners can be safe with one another only when they are safe with the teacher and in the learning environment.

A simple mode of safety is laughter. "No laughter, no learning!" Frankly, I wondered for years why this axiom was so true and helpful. Now I see that laughter—healthy, deep laughter—is not only a sign of safety, but also a means of making learners feel and be safe. Laughter coming from a classroom or lab, lecture hall or workshop is, for me, an indicator of learning that is sound and social.

In any learning situation of significance, learners must be given to understand that there is no one right answer. Otherwise, we present education as a giant guessing game. I am troubled deeply when I see adult learners subjected to closed questions, while the teacher goes on a grand fishing expedition. There is a mystery at the heart of any human discipline; that's what keeps us scientists searching relentlessly. When that mystery is approached in a safe learning environment, there is no end to learning.

Safety involves the challenge of dissent. Learners of any age must dissent somewhat before they can truly contextualize and construct the skills, knowledge, and attitudes they are learning for their life. Dissent is not disrespect. A teacher who welcomes dissent, who rises to the challenge not of defending but of exploring what he is teaching, is, in my mind, a true scientist.

Both personal learning styles (http://www.vark-learn.com) and psychological types (http://www.humanmetrics.com/) demonstrate how idiosyncratic one's response to the principle of safety is. This principle opens the way for learners to meet any challenge, and it wisely cleanses the environment of the destructive element of fear. Challenge is not fear. Fear stops learning, freezes creativity and spontaneity, shuts down laughter, and destroys community. It is what we find in the dark classrooms of Charles Dickens's time. It is never appropriate in a dialogue education setting.

Safety On-Line

Clear and discrete parameters, access to facilitators and mentors, a system of speedy response to questions, well-designed learning tasks—all serve to make the on-line learning environment safe. Safety is not an end in itself in either on-line or face-to-face learning. It is a factor in the learning environment that enhances learning, as sunlight, rain, and clean air nourish plants in a garden. I expect research will disclose that the main reasons adults leave a course or learning situation is that they do not feel safe. "Who needs it?" they say, and they go back to their lives as they were.

Note how all of these principles of sound learning relate directly to structures. Clear and discrete parameters provide safety through the seven design steps, wherein learners see exactly what this unit will teach and the achievement-based objectives (ABOs). Mentors and facilitators are as good as the learners' access to them. Initially in an on-line course, that may be somewhat asynchronous, and it may feel like the instructor is on duty 24/7. A system of clear parameters can deal with this opening burden on generous professors: *My chat room is open on Fridays from 2:00 to 6:00 PM and I will respond to e-mail questions within twenty-four hours.* Once a pattern is established and explicitly reviewed, it can be a place of safety for all.

A system of speedy response to process or content questions is an assurance of safety in an on-line course. A thorough response offered within twenty-four hours of the request or question is evidence, not only to the questioner but to the whole group, that the course leader is serious about safety. Notice that such a response touches on respect, immediacy, clear roles, and accountability. None of these principles works alone.

Sound Relationships

This principle involves respect, a keen interest in the perspective of the other, and empathy for the struggle that real learning involves. Through the LNRA, the learner in an event meets the professor or trainer early on and has time to take her measure. The soundness of the learning relationship is a function of the soundness of the person who claims to teach. Nothing less.

Adult learners in any situation are much like children in their acuity, their quick ability to judge truth from falseness, their inability to put up with facile talk and empty show. One of the great advantages of using dialogue education is the need for congruence. If you do not do it, you cannot teach it. Again, we have come to realize that the dialogue in dialogue education is not between teacher and learner, but among learners, of whom the teacher is one, in her own mind. Because in dialogue education everyone is learning, there is a constant holding of one another's feet to the fire. So the openness and clarity of the teacher—who admits to learning and growing within an event and shows behavioral indicators of such learning—is the means of putting this principle of sound relationships into play.

The teacher must be a certain distance from learners to enhance their learning. Even as he meets the learners, surveys their needs and resources, researches their context, and teaches them, he is most useful when there is a certain detachment present. The teacher is not responsible for their learning; they are. He is responsible to them to prepare, to make well-designed programs and materials, to set learning tasks, and respond to questions with competence and grace. But he is not a "friend" unless they want a friend who will hold their feet to the fire as need be. That is his role. Clarity about that is another source of the soundness in our relationship.

Sound Relationships On-Line

All that we have considered so far applies, of course, in an on-line situation. Sound relationships among learners, between learners and teacher, are perhaps even more necessary in the virtual world of on-line learning. In the on-line course I took recently, the professor offered a wise suggestion to ensure the maintenance of sound relationships: write your e-mail in Word, then cut and paste it into the e-mail program. This gives you time to review what you have written so you are not sending out words you might later want to retract. Another way to do this is to set up your e-mail program with a two-step send: first to the outbox, then send. A third way is to save the message in the drafts folder until you're satisfied with what you've written.

One learner's perspective. Here is what I, as learner, need when I sign up to study with a professor in an on-line course. I need to know his competencies, his strengths, and the boundaries of his knowledge. I need to see behaviors that indicate his respect for me, his interest in my context and in my perspective, and his empathy for my struggle to learn. I need unambiguous directions about learning tasks and resources, and I need access to him, especially at the beginning of a course, to make sure that I understand printed directives. I am a physical learner: until I do it, I do not know how to do it. Perhaps there are others like me out there. Here is where every set of directions can be tested from the perspective of a visual, auditory, and kinesthetic learner. I also need affirmation from the teacher along the way, to keep me on board. As an extrovert, I find virtual responses pale replications of the face-to-face or voice interaction I need. Someday, the prevalence of web cams will supply that quasi-physical support. Today, my on-line teachers will have to be creative in ascertaining true inclusion, encouragement, and sustained motivation to ensure a sound relationship for learning.

I admit that all this seems unduly demanding of the weary teacher of an on-line course. I can only promise to provide such service when I am leading an on-line course because I know that's what learning demands.

Sequence and Reinforcement

The previous safety principle speaks to congruent behaviors of teachers in a learning event; sequence and reinforcement speaks to the design of materials and learning tasks. If you fail to honor this principle of sequence, you will find learners confused. Fail to provide reinforcement in their learning tasks and you risk losing them all together.

By sequence I mean the order of events: small to large, simple to complex, easy to difficult. This principle gives the teacher or designer of dialogue education courses, workshops, trainings, and classes a dependable barometer: how does this sequence enable them to learn? We are still demanding hard work of learners—we ask for an ongoing struggle to master language, skills, concepts, behaviors—but we do so supported by the gentle framework of a thoughtful sequence.

When a learner has missed a lecture or some vital input, we establish a system of peer mentoring so that the sequence of presentations is not broken. When a group of learners clearly has difficulty with a concept or practice, we retreat. We go back through the system and try it "once more with feeling."

Kofi Annan of the United Nations made a wise observation about the diverse methods of different disciplines. He commented,

> When a scientist conducts a thousand experiments before finding the precise formula for a new drug, we pay him well for all the time spent and celebrate his efforts. When statesmen spent hours in negotiations and at the end come out with a peace treaty, we ask, "Why did it take you so long?" [*The Charlie Rose Show*, March 12, 2006]

A respectful sequence in the materials and processes in any discipline is a central principle of dialogue education. One can look at a seven step design and see the sequence. If the sequence is not appropriate, it will be evident in the response of learners to the tasks.

Time for an Appropriate Sequence

There are three important elements that make dialogue education work, in this order: time, time, and time. Human beings need time to learn. We need time for reflection as well as practical implementation of new content. So the sequence of learning tasks must take into account this new awareness of the importance of time. Notice that the *When?* (time frame) design step precedes, in sequence, the choice of *What?* (content).

When education is seen as a presentation of a sequenced set of facts and information, the time element is managed by the presenter. He needs enough time to "cover" the material. Therefore, the time allocated to learning events is usually short. One can take only so much "covering."

When we use dialogue education, time is a measure not only of content but also of process. We insist that learning take place *in* the event, not after the event. We insist on learning tasks with four parts, one of which is implementation—whereby learners, as we have seen, do something relevant and immediately useful with the new content.

Teaching can be done in a shorter time frame than learning. Frankly, this is a vital factor in the difference between the two. We know that no two people learn in the same way; however, this element of time is vital no matter what your learning style.

Reinforcement

Reinforcement is a form of sequence whereby learning tasks offer new and different applications of the concept, skill, or attitudes being learned. How many times must one reinforce a complex concept or skill? If not just teaching but also learning occurs within a class, as it is designed to do in dialogue education, then this is a strategic question for any teacher. If inclusion is significant, and no one is excluded from the learning potential, I as teacher must work very hard indeed to make the right judgment about reinforcement.

Creative reinforcement is delightful to all. We are not talking about *repetition*. Repetition can be used to prepare students for examinations; however, that's not the kind of reinforcement meant here. A brilliant young head teacher at a charter school in a small town in North Carolina says, "We do not teach to the tests [No Child Left Behind federal examinations]—our children learn way beyond the tests" (William Friday interview, *PBS*, March 22, 2006).

You know the content (the *What?*) to be learned. It is up to you to design enough different and diverse ways to do something with that content so the whole group learns *How* do they know they know? You will observe the behaviors that they are using and that they will use in their own context—as transfer of the learning.

I cannot but wonder if the C– in mathematics that I earned in my first year at university might not have been an A had the good professor known dialogue education. His sequence was telescoped and *f-a-s-t*; I can hear him saying, "I have so much to cover this term, I have to move through everything at this speedy clip." There were no systems for mentoring laggards, and there was little reinforcement as we moved at a lightning pace from one mathematical complexity to the next.

Peer mentoring, small-group work around learning tasks, portfolio analysis by the teacher, extended research on the computer, help stations in the room staffed by aides or other students—these are all forms of reinforcement. As teachers and learners work together, creative methods of reinforcement emerge.

Sequence and Reinforcement On-Line

These principles are relevant to the design of on-line materials, learning tasks, and systems for learning. When a teacher or course designer is thinking about sequence and reinforcement, he is thinking about learning and designing for it.

In asynchronous work, the learner can go back over the sequence of learning tasks and see how one thing leads to another, how it is moving from small to large, simple to complex, hard to difficult. When the teacher and learners enter the synchronous world, their celebration of the complexity, difficulty, and sheer size of the work can be encouraging and motivating. Reinforcement can support an autonomous learner who can create for himself learning tasks that assure him of his mastery of a concept. However, here is where the teacher's affirmation, support, encouragement, celebration are vital. It is so easy to be overwhelmed at the first struggling attempt. It is not only the teacher who must watch for these indicators. Because dialogue education is social, mentors and small groups and peer systems are vital to support competent learning.

A daily on-line report card from learners—on process as well as on personal and small-group competence with the content, on materials and supplementary research guides—could be useful. This is entirely possible on-line. This can be a means of hearing the pleas of laggards like me or of celebrating the speed of those who are moving along. This sort of formative evaluation can be a way of creative reinforcement of not only effective learning but also the systems that enhance it. In the on-line course I took at University of Detroit Mercy, the student's logbook was a source of data for formative evaluation.

The deep purpose of these principles of sequence and reinforcement is protection: to ensure that no one, because of confusion or a loss of confidence, excludes herself from the learning process. How many adults dropped out of an education program or an on-line course yesterday? Assiduous attention to sequencing of content and process, and careful, creative reinforcement might well prevent that expensive loss.

Praxis: Action with Reflection

Praxis is a Greek word that means action with reflection. It stands as a warning against academic verbiage that concentrates on elusive and often esoteric concepts as though the abstract concepts were the reality. According to Plato, they *are* the reality. Therefore, praxis serves insofar as it makes new content relevant to learners, as they re-create or construct that content to transform their life and context.

Praxis invites us as teachers to construct learning tasks that move learners to reflection on the topic being taught. Inductive work in a learning task connects the topic to their life and context. The input task offers new content and then, in the implementation section, learners are challenged to do something meaningful with that new content. That doing must involve reflection on the revelation of that new content to themselves, to their life and context. As the novelist E. M. Forster advises, "Only connect."

Recently, a professor at a large western university wrote to me: "I teach computer science, so I do not see how dialogue enters into my classes. There is nothing to discuss."

When the manual of the machine becomes a catechism, we are in trouble. Dialogue education is not a discussion about computers, but a way for young technocrats to learn not only the technology, but also the sociology, the anthropology, the philosophy, the history, and the politics of computer use.

The creative imagination is a large factor in praxis: *What would happen if . . . What are the implications of . . . How do you see these programs in twenty years . . . ?* Reflection can become "pre-flection"—a look forward as well as inward.

The word *exercise* is misleading following an input of new content. We are not doing exercises or activities to see how well learners have grasped a theory or skill. In designing and using learning tasks, we are inviting them to grapple with that theory and skill, to make it theirs and to make it fit their life and context. That is constructed knowing.

It is a tribute when educators tell me, "I took the seven design steps and made them into quite a different model for the specific group of learners I was teaching." Any theory worth its salt is worth changing.

Praxis On-Line

In the University of Detroit Mercy on-line course, a major task was for young educators to design a personal portfolio and a website they could use for job searches in future. This task was set on day one, and it was clear that whatever was written initially would be considered and rewritten many times over the course of the program. This presented an ongoing praxis.

Every learning task set on-line can be praxis, demanding creative reflection on the virtually infinite resources of the World Wide Web. Without such praxis, learning tasks would invite collections of information. That is not constructed knowing. That would be a facile response to Paulo Freire's query, "What is *to know?*"

Using Ideas/Feelings/Actions

This principle is based on the premise that the best learning is threefold: cognitive, affective, and psychomotor; that is, it involves ideas, feelings, and actions. Thus we relate to personal learning styles—visual, auditory, read/write, and kinesthetic—as well as to personal type. How can we incorporate all these considerations into a learning task? This principle guides us by inviting cognitive action, feelings, and some muscle work. Each learner has to identify with that part of the lesson that most appeals to him. However, he *can* do what is not his preference, and *will* do when his preferred aspect is included. Again, the principle is a protection against self-exclusion. When there is nothing in a course or seminar or lesson or workshop that speaks directly to the learner, he or she will not learn.

I am a kinesthetic learner on the VARK scale (visual, auditory, read/write, kinesthetic; see www.vark-learn.com) and an ENFP on the Myers-Briggs scale (Kiersey and Hatch, 1998). I can listen to lectures (auditory), and watch PowerPoint presentations (visual). I read and write well (read/write) and learn by doing that. I can work alone and think through a problem to come to a new insight. But put me into a hands-on situation (kinesthetic), in a small group, and I fly into new learning. Preference means just that. When the teacher intentionally includes cognitive, affective, and psychomotor aspects in a learning task, there is something for everyone's preference.

We know that we teach to our own preferences. This principle protects us teachers from our own predilections, from shaping all learning as if we were the prototypical student and the only type present. Notice how the fourfold aspect of a learning task includes reinforcement of cognitive, affective, and psychomotor work. Learners can read new ideas, write their impressions or reflections, identify the affective application of these ideas (*What would it feel like . . .*), and then do something with the ideas: create a collage, do computer or library research, build a model, do laboratory testing. Such teaching is fail-safe, in the best sense of the word.

Ideas/Feelings/Actions On-Line

Other aspects of dialogue education can ascertain that this principle and practice is at work in on-line study. The seven design steps demand solid, substantive, well-researched *What?* content. The next step (*What for?*) demands that we consider tough, working verbs for the ABOs. Incorporating feelings or the affective aspect into on-line work calls for utmost creativity. There is no such thing as a *virtual* feeling. Feelings are always real and often operative in the success or failure of learning. What feelings were involved that brought an adult learner to the decision to give up on an on-line course? Designing a sound system of peer mentoring and small-group work is one obvious route to this affective aspect. Personal attention from the professor in large class situations is often difficult but never goes unrewarded. Again, a system for this is invaluable. "Friday evening check-in" is what one professor has devised. His students talk to him via e-mail every Friday evening about their status in the course and their feelings about what they are learning. The daily unit report card mentioned earlier can also be framed in terms of learners' feelings about their learning.

Here is a research agenda for all of us: how do we get the human touch into the virtual world? Without that human touch, our purpose in learning can be torn asunder. We learn to make better bombs instead of how to make a world without them.

Constructivism. When these principles are in play, we can expect learners to construct theory and skills that are appropriate to their context. Because a learning task involves learning within the event—the course, the seminar, the training, the program, and transfer of that learning to the learner's life situation—that transfer has a good chance of being contextualized, of being appropriate. One is not simply practicing a skill or identifying the use of a concept. One is using what was learned in a way appropriate to one's own context. This is an immediacy of application.

Respect for Learners as Decision Makers

A central principle in dialogue education is consistent respect for learners as decision makers in their own learning. Dialogue that is fruitful of learning is always between subjects or decision makers. There is no dialogue when one considers the other the object of his teaching. We often call what we teach the *subject*. In fact, it is the *object*, and the other, the learner, is—as you are—a subject in the dialogue *about* that object.

When we are in intense dialogue—learning together as subjects the knowledge, skills, and attitudes that are meaningful to our context—we bring that content to life. This is what occurs in an effective learning task when the content is restructured by the honest dialogue of learners and teacher. This is respect manifest for all involved and for the content being taught.

Example

This is a two-hour session on distributive justice for a church group of adults considering reform of the health care system.

What? (content):

1. What is distributive justice?
2. How can the concept help us see the allocation of resources for health care?

What for? (objectives): By the end of these two hours all will have

1. Reasonably defined distributive justice
2. Examined the history of health care in our state
3. Reviewed upcoming legislation on the issue

How? (learning tasks): Note the respect for learners as subjects in this task:

Learning Task 1: Defining Distributive Justice
In pairs, read these definitions of distributive justice. Circle what strikes you as important in those definitions. We'll hear all that you circled.

> Distributive justice concerns what is just or right with respect to the allocation of goods in a society. Thus, a community whose individual members are rendered their due would be considered a society guided by the principles of distributive justice. Often contrasted with procedural justice, which is concerned with just processes such as in the administration of law, distributive justice concentrates on just outcomes and consequences. The most prominent contemporary theorist of distributive justice is the philosopher John Rawls.
>
> Distributive justice considers the distribution of goods among members of society at a specific time and, on that basis, determines whether the state of affairs is acceptable. For example, someone who evaluates a situation by looking at the standard of living, absolute wealth, wealth disparity, or any other such utilitarian standard, is thinking in terms of distributive justice. Generally, those people who hold egalitarianism to be important, even implicitly, rely on notions of distributive justice.

However, not all advocates of consequentialist theories are concerned with an equitable society. What unites them is the mutual interest in achieving the best possible results or, in terms of the preceding example, the most perfect distribution of wealth. [http://en.wikipedia.org/wiki/Distributive_justice]

Learning Task 2: History of Health Care in Our State

2A. Watch these videos from http://www.citizenshealthcare .gov/. As you watch, write your questions and comments, and share them in a small group of six.

2B. Name in your group one way distributive justice applies to this problem of health care reform. We'll hear from each group.

Notice in the example that the application of the theory to the problem as depicted in the video affects the theory. Distributive justice, as defined by the resources, is not what learners have learned. They have constructed their own meaning through the dialogue. The resources are not rejected or refused; learners have applied the given definitions to their real life context. This gives a new quality to the original object of the study.

Men and women will act as subjects (decision makers) on new content, constructing it to serve their context, when engaged in learning through dialogue.

Immediacy

The learning needs and resources assessment is a tool toward immediacy—making sure that the learning is designed to fit the life and context of the learners. Learning is not therapy, but good learning is therapeutic. It is not our job as teachers to meet all needs or solve all problems. However, it is our job to make the new content—ideas, skills, attitudes—meaningful to learners. The premise here is that learners will respond to content that has immediate usefulness to their life and context.

Freire spoke of generative themes; that is, themes or ideas that generate energy because they resonate with learners. Talk to the white-haired seniors at our church about their grandchildren, talk to high school boys about high school girls, and watch their faces flush, their eyes light up, their words come pouring out. Dialogue revolves around the generative themes of the learners. Teachers and preachers talk to us often about *their* themes. It is our difficult task as teachers to design lessons with immediacy, with direct relevance to the generative themes of the learners themselves.

The professor of information technology said, "No place for dialogue here." I disagree. The young people he is teaching are bubbling with IT themes. It is his job to discover them and to make them work for learning. The first part of a learning task, remember, is inductive work—anchoring new learning to the life and context of learners. This is where we use or invoke their themes. For example, teaching a high school class how to use a new edition of Microsoft Word, one invites the young people to write and print a short love letter to their girlfriend or boyfriend. Teaching those grandparents to use the same software, one can invite them to write to their grandchildren, in a bold, forty-six-point font. Creativity is the challenge here. Without immediacy, a class pales. Just as I need to have some aspect of the learning task relate to my preferences, I must see the connection of the new learning to life, my life and context. Unless the dialogue begins long before the learning event does, such connection is hard to achieve.

Once again, we see the interrelation of all the facets of dialogue education: seven design steps, LNRA, learning tasks in four parts, and these principles and practices. Teaching is a social science, and the quantum principle holds: the whole is greater than the sum of its parts, and the whole is in each of its parts. Again, E. M. Forster's admonition speaks loudly to us in relation to immediacy: "Only connect."

Immediacy On-Line

An on-line course has great potential for immediacy through the feedback technology and the opportunity for synchronous relations with a group of people. The immediacy of theme and content is another story, and all that has been said already about this vital principle holds for on-line teaching.

Since men and women taking an on-line course are often working as well as studying, they can apply new learning directly to this work context, consider what it means and what it does, and write about that. This is praxis, and it is the use of the principle of immediacy on-line.

Through appropriate learning tasks, learners on-line can take responsibility to make clear and explicit the potential relevance of new content to their context. That is the job of both the implementation and integration parts of a learning task. These move the learner to test a theory in a familiar context and to use a skill appropriately at home or at work. This is both sound learning and a cogent, immediate transfer of learning.

Clear Roles

This principle is as much a management principle as an epistemological one. It tells us that the role of teacher must be spelled out explicitly and clearly, and the role of each person in a learning group must be defined as well. When roles are clear, the work of learning gets done. Ambiguity of role is a powerful scapegoat: *I did not know you wanted me to do that!* Who sets the task? Who is the timekeeper? Who makes the lunch? Who washes up? Who is to document the results of our dialogue? When these questions are answered up front and clearly, learning is effective.

Many failures occur in a learning team because of ambiguity or lack of clarity: *I thought you were doing that!* Here we see how structure in dialogue education is a service to learning. It provides not only a framework, but also, again, protection against wasted time, frustration, confusion, and failure to get the learning job done.

For example, in a recent training workshop, my colleague and I had ascribed specific tasks to each of us. Our roles and responsibilities were spelled out in detail to prevent any confusion or ambiguity. Then without warning, one of the older adult learn-ers showed serious signs of fatigue and dehydration, complaining of dizziness. My colleague and I looked across the table at one another, and she stood up to take Mr. J. out of the room to the foyer, where she got him water and a cup of tea, and led him to a comfortable chair where he could sleep for a bit. I stepped into her role and responsibility because it had been so clearly spelled out beforehand. We did not lose a beat in the progress of the workshop.

The clearer the role of teacher and learners, the more precise the demands of that role, the more complete the learning. The teacher is, for example, a resource, not a mere "presenter" of infor-mation, not the one with the answers. Each member of the learn-ing group has a role within that group, and as each can become clear about his or her role, learning moves along. Had I been teaching alone in the situation with Mr. J., I would have nodded to a senior student to take the role of caretaker. Can you see where the relationships built along the way are valuable to all?

Clear Roles On-Line

How a mentor team works will depend on the clarity of role specifi-cation. How learning tasks are completed and reported will depend on the clarity of directions: who does what by when? When there is ambiguity in role expectations on-line, there is lost energy, frus-tration, and blocked learning. How a chat room works for the development of learning skills for all will depend on the clarity and simplicity of directions. The University of Detroit Mercy has a very useful, accessible set of guidelines (http://www.comput-ease .net/teaching-learning/discussion.htm).

Teamwork

In dialogue education, most learning tasks are completed in small groups, even if some work is done individually. The better the small group works together, the better the learning for all. In every small group I have worked in, there has been my "other"—not a doppelganger or twin but, on the contrary, the person whose skills and preferences are opposite to mine. She is probably an ISTJ on the Myers-Briggs scale, quite different from my ENFP. I will have the big-picture idea, the vision for how this learning task can be accomplished; she will lay out the steps and do the math and take care of the details.

This is synchronicity at work. One does not plan such a conjunction of types in a team. But the small group, working together to get the learning task accomplished and the tough learning under its belt, can count on diverse gifts and preferences. Our part is to celebrate them, acknowledge them, and welcome their input.

Pity the learning team that is made up of all one type: ENFP, kinesthetic learners—you can see what a disadvantage that can be. The four or six people at a table doing a learning task will invariably present a variety of preferences and types.

For example, at a rehabilitation hospital course on setting up one's home for safety after surgery, I was in a small group with peers who were all as terrified as I was. Had the learning task been set as *Name items in your home that might be dangerous if you were using a walker,* I would have named the danger of fire from the stove; another might have named slippery rugs or movable side tables. Together, from our diverse perspectives, we could have named a complete list. Instead, the rehab specialist told us her list of items we had to be careful about, and the list was remarkably incomplete and wrong for our idiosyncratic contexts. A powerful axiom of dialogue education says: *Never do for a learner what she can do for herself.*

There is safety in a learning team. Sound relationships in the team reflect the model of the relationship between the teacher and learners. Team members will work together using their minds, hearts, and hands, as the learning tasks demand; they will discover that mutual respect makes the work go well. In short, the learning team is a microcosm for the use of all of these principles and practices.

When there is apparent trouble in a learning team, I make it my policy as teacher to stay away from it until the very last moment. I have seen men and women work things out over time and discover that their learning was not only of the named content, but also of how to work things out in the team, over time. Many learners have told me that the named content was in fact an indirect route to the actual content of the team's learning.

It is our task, as teachers, to be aware of the tensions and struggles of a learning team, and to intervene when necessary. I have learned that such intervention is best attempted at the last possible moment, not when I first discern difficulty. *"Do not steal the learning moment from the learning group"*—that's the axiom that fits here.

An Example of Teamwork. I offer a three-hour workshop entitled *A Taste of Dialogue Education for Peace*, which is sponsored by our Raleigh Chapter of the Fellowship of Reconciliation (www.forusa.org). Even in the design of such an event, teamwork enters to enhance the learning of all. My colleague is a detail person. I call on her strong suit to balance mine: she reviews the materials and catches my most egregious errors. Teamwork! In the course, small groups struggle with the demands of dialogue education, and I can observe the balancing of big-idea folk and pragmatic-detail folk. The learning product manifests this teamwork.

Again, the other principles and practices come into play in small-group work: safety, engagement, sequence and reinforcement, respect for the other as subject of her own learning. These principles are each part of a whole.

Teamwork On-Line

The virtual world is a great site for tough teamwork. Inviting learners to do research and write a paper together is a small-group challenge worthy of the name. Here is where roles and responsibilities must be explicit and crystal clear. Timelines, sequence of steps and deadlines, a system for immediate feedback—all this makes dialogue education on-line work to enhance learning.

Engagement

Unless the learner is engaged—physically, mentally, emotionally engaged—we are not doing dialogue education. The purpose, remember, is learning. The goal, remember, is equity, peace, and the end of domination systems. When learners are engaged, they must be engaged at the level of criticism and construction of theory. It is not enough to engage adult learners in repetition of the teacher's perceptions. A learner can as well learn to hate in that mode. By engagement I mean a wrestling with a theory, a struggle with a skill, a resistant practice of a difficult attitude. Acceptance and docility are not virtues in dialogue education. Engagement is manifest in the questioning glance, the screwed-up forehead, the shaking head, the shock at the challenge a learning task presents.

I sometimes turn to a public service TV station that presents courses being taught at a local university. The postures of disengagement of undergraduates are worthy of note. Where else, in our lives, do we sit quietly and listen, without opportunities for engagement? Using dialogue education, we can present that same lecture and see physical signs of engagement as individuals summarize main topics and small groups get to work to unpack the lecture, to question it, to critique it, to implement—in ways appropriate to their context—the new content. This is not "a discussion group searching for the right answers." This is dialogue; this is transformative learning (Mezirow, 1991).

Remember, we call the tasks *learning* tasks. One part of the learning task is reflection on the new input, that which is added, new content. Then learners must engage with that content and, with the teacher of the content, make it theirs.

Tom Sappington, a brilliant teacher and friend, put it this way: "I see. In good learning, we set the table well, with succulent, nutritious, and visually delightful morsels. Then we let the learners select, taste, and digest for themselves." That is the level of engagement and autonomy we need for dialogue education.

Joye Norris speaks of the moment when learners find their voice (Norris, 2003). A learning task is set, and a small group starts out somewhat timidly to complete it. One after another speaks to the issue; slowly their experience and power come alive and they find their voice in the dialogue. She invites us to listen to the change of tone in the room as that occurs.

Until that occurs, learners can be passive, empty vessels, in a process that Belenky and her colleagues, in *Women's Ways of Knowing* (Belenky, Clinchy, Goldberger, and Tarule, 1997b), call *received knowing*. The learners accept what they hear from a learned teacher, without question, critique, or passion. Knowledge is "passed on"— tradition—and I propose that this is nothing less than dangerous. My tradition is not necessarily appropriate for men and women of another culture, whether in the Bronx or Bucharest or Burundi. Learners have to engage with new content to make it valued and valuable to them. One does not learn how to do that except by doing it consistently, continually, systematically.

At a recent event where I offered a dialogue education keynote, an older teacher who had read many of my earlier books said, at the end of the session, "Well, I had read the lyrics. Now, I have heard the music." He was talking about the symphony of learning he had heard in the room, as his colleagues engaged in learning tasks around their issues.

A delightful dilemma faced by dialogue education teachers, professors, and leaders arises at the moment when you wish to bring small groups back to the large group for synthesis work, or reflection on their learning, or closure of a learning task. Often, you cannot get their attention! This is one of the highlights of my professional life: people are so deeply engaged in learning they will not pay attention to the teacher.

Engagement On-Line

An on-line course can be an opportunity for intense personal and group engagement. When dialogue education structures and systems are used, such engagement is visible, measurable, and productive. Learners not only construct theory to fit their life and context, but they also produce new materials that are sound indicators of their learning.

Accountability

We as designers, teachers, professors or facilitators of workshops are accountable to the learner to do what we propose in our seven step design. This is why learners are expected to review the course book at the beginning of a course or session. It is our contract. They have informed it by their responses to the LNRA. They subscribe to the contract by their presence in the course. I am accountable both to them and to the content. When it says in the *What for?* (ABOs) that "participants will have . . ." it is the teacher's job to make sure that what is contracted occurs.

Therefore, the teacher has no right to go off on a tangent, no matter how brilliant a tangent it is. He has no right to omit a learning task or cut a program short. He has no "lectern" here to express his opinions on the subject. He is accountable. Such accountability is the heart of dialogue education. Such accountability is what students celebrate when they leave a course knowing that they know (Vella, 2001). Such accountability is a function of the intense and assiduous preparation that dialogue education demands.

Learners are of course accountable as well. Their accountability is not to the teacher or to the federal or state testers. Their accountability is to themselves and to their peers as they work in small groups. They are accountable for their own learning.

In the dialogue education paradigm, teachers are in a service learning relationship to learners. Happily, we see learners serving one another in such an environment, assisting, mentoring one another. Structure and safety, these sound principles, and the scholarship within the input section of a learning task provide energy for the struggle to learn complex theory, demanding skills, and new attitudes.

For example, I had the pleasure recently of preparing a set of one-hour courses as an introduction to the philosophy of the French theologian Teilhard de Chardin, for our Faith and Science program at our Episcopal church. Chardin's thought, as offered in his books *The Phenomenon of Man* and *The Divine Milieu*, is complex and demanding. The seven step design set the good folk to work on learning tasks featuring input from these two books. These adult learners were stunned by how difficult the tasks were; at the same time, they were honored by the challenge. Some begged, "Please, just *tell us* what this all means." But others recognized the potential of really learning Teilhard's message by working hard together. They left the first session tired and somewhat confused, but they came back. As we struggled together with the material over the next few weeks, these men and women began to construct Teilhard's thought for themselves in a way that fit their lives and contexts. Accountability for a dialogue educator means doing the hard thing—not telling, but teaching so people learn.

These adult learners were in turn accountable to the content as they struggled with it, and to one another as they listened to questions and responses based on a first reading of the material. Ultimately, the learner is accountable to himself. Ultimately, we learn alone, and such learning is enhanced and supported by our work in the group. The group members are accountable to one another to ensure that no one is excluded from the learning. But we do learn alone.

Accountability On-Line

In the University of Detroit Mercy on-line course, the first visible accountability was that of the designer and professor, who was forthright in setting out her goals for the course. The well-wrought and assiduously prepared structure and materials manifested that accountability. We learners were accountable to take part in discussion chat rooms on specific issues, and to complete all assignments. The more involved the learner becomes, the more she learns.

In a traditional college classroom, each person can be an island. The professor, lectures, questions, tests, and grades individual students who read, do assignments, and take examinations. I went through a graduate program in English literature in the sixties at a famous university in New York City without ever meeting or talking with another graduate student. That isolation is not possible in the on-line course as designed by the University of Detroit Mercy. That virtual world was actually friendlier than the New York real one.

I believe a mentoring system in an on-line situation can be another source of mutual accountability. Mentors can work together, share problems and concerns, and grow in skills and knowledge in a virtual, symbiotic relationship.

I have named this section on the twelve selected principles "Sound." An old axiom of health is *Mens sana in corpore sano*: a sound mind in a sound body. *Sana* reminds me of the word *sane*. These principles can make teaching and learning sane in an insane world, where some of the best instruction globally is in the armed services on how to kill and how to use weapons of destruction. Dialogue education offers the antithesis to this: one sound way to construct a world where war is obsolete and peace is the law of the globe, where sanity rules in education through a set of sound principles and practices.

Implementation Challenge 6A: Face-to-Face

Consider a recent course you took or taught. Consider these twelve basic principles and practices of dialogue education: learning needs and resources assessment, safety, sound relationships, sequence and reinforcement, praxis, respect, ideas/feelings/actions, immediacy, clear roles, teamwork, engagement, accountability.

In what one way would you revise the design of that course by including one or more of these?

Implementation Challenge 6B: On-Line

Many of us have visited a chat room during an on-line course or added our thoughts to a discussion thread. Consider one way in which at least one of these dialogue education principles and practices could enhance your participation in such an on-line dialogue.

7

OPEN QUESTIONS INVITE DIALOGUE

The simple tactic of *asking open questions* in educational design can become a strategy. Open questions do invite dialogue. There is no more powerful tool to stimulate authentic, constructed knowing and vigorous learning. *A learning task is an open question put to a small group with all the resources they need to respond.*

Open questions elicit the power of context and life. The open question assumes respect for learners and for their experience and current knowledge. Open questions often begin with How: *How would this theory work in my setting? How will I teach this skill to my colleagues? How will this help me respond to my problematic situation? How does this all relate to my life and context?*

When an open question has been asked of a group, it is imperative that the teacher sit still, be quiet, and pay attention. There is a great temptation to respond ourselves to the question just posed. This can mean our stealing the learning opportunity from the learners. The quiet that occurs before dialogue around a meaningful open question is sacred and essential to their learning.

Closed Questions

Most of us have spent a great deal of our lives as school-based learners responding to closed questions. In church school, the catechism did not even put the answer at the back of the book: it was right there! That "learning" involved question and response—repeat the question, give the printed response.

Whose learning were we learning? In those classrooms, all disciplines had the textbook with the pink cover (teacher's edition) with the answers to all the tests in the back. Little wonder we grew up as linear thinkers, knowing for certain that there was one answer and it was in the back of the (pink) book.

In some bleak pedagogical archive there must be a text describing a method of teaching that looks much like *fishing*. The teacher says: *Today we will cover the political geography of Europe. What is the capital of the United Kingdom? And of France? Of Germany? Of Belgium?*

At this moment, classes in university, community college, and technical schools are beginning with a set of fishing questions. This behavior is as far from dialogue education as is possible. These are not open questions, but closed questions with a sting of domination. *I know; you do not know.*

From Closed to Open Questions

London was indeed the capital of England and Paris of France— but how did that happen? Why London? Why Paris? What is the relation of one to the other? What would have been the effect of making a coastal town in France the capital city, or of making Belfast the capital of the UK? How does this dialogue relate to the Middle East and the issue of Jerusalem? Imagine the difference in the quality of dialogue and of learning with this kind of thinking: the opposite of linear thinking. Such open questions invite connected, circular, profound, open thinking. Dana Zohar (1997) suggests this is *quantum thinking*. She explains these differences through quantum physics in terms of three functions of the brain: the one-to-one leap of energy between neurons on a neural tract, which she calls *serial thinking*; the leap of energy in a pattern across a neural network, which she calls *patterned* or *associative thinking*; and the explosion of energy throughout the whole brain using a network of neural networks, which she names *quantum thinking*.

Here are some examples.

Serial thinking: What is the capital of Portugal? The capital of Portugal is Lisbon.

Patterned thinking: What do you notice about many of the capital cities of Europe? Many of the capitals of Europe are on waterways.

Quantum thinking: Political and economic realities are and have always been deeply entwined. Notice that all of the capitals of Europe are on waterways. How is the Internet, which we are using for this course, a global waterway? Where do you think the capital of the Internet lies?

Open questions are involved in patterned and quantum thinking.

Teaching as dialogue invites quantum thinking and quantum learning (Vella, 2002). It is the transformational learning that Mezirow (1991) defined. The quality of such learning may be one cogent answer to current problems in education at every level. The open question does not belittle facts and figures; it moves directly to examine them, to analyze the connections, and to consider the implications. Whatever you are teaching, a linear recital of facts and figures is hardly worth the effort. The definition of a learning task includes reference to open questions. *A learning task is an open question put to a small group with all the resources they need to respond.* The resources (facts and figures) can be incontrovertible data. However, this is *not* what you are teaching. Such data is available on the Internet with a flick of the finger: go to Google or to any search engine with the right question. Here are examples of data:

Over thirty thousand humans have been killed in the Iraq war.

China's population in 2007 is estimated to be 1,321,851,888.

Mozart composed twelve operas from 1767 to 1791.

The seven design steps of dialogue education are *Who? Why? When? Where? What? What for?* and *How?*

The content of your teaching is not mere data or information, but the meaning of that information in a particular context.

Testing is often an examination of learners' retention of data. It often involves serial thinking. Evaluation in dialogue education is not testing: it is rather an examination and evaluation of behavioral indicators that show constructed, quantum knowing (see Part Four, Sure).

Examples

Here are two dialogue education designs showing quantum knowing that includes serial and patterned knowing.

Dialogue Education Lesson 1: The Fatalities of the Iraq War 2003–2007

What? (content):

>Thousands of men, women, and children have died in this Iraq war (2003–2007).

What for? (achievement-based objectives):

>By the end of this class, all will have

- Calculated the cost of the Iraq war in human lives; examined pictures of the dead.
- Identified contemporaries among them.
- Composed a short letter to the family of a contemporary killed in this war.

How? (learning tasks and materials):

- Examine these charts of up-to-date data at your table.
- Look at these sets of pictures of war dead: Iraqi and Coalition forces.
- Identify contemporaries: men and women your own age.
- Compose a short letter from your table group to that person's family.

Dialogue Education Lesson 2: China's Population Growth 2007

What? (content):

China's population in 2007 is estimated to be 1,321,900,000

What for? (achievement-based objectives):

By the end of this class all will have

- Identified on a map of China the areas of most rapid growth.
- Named strengths and problems in this growth pattern.

How? (learning tasks to be done in small groups):

- Examine this graph of China's population in 2007.
- Identify on the wall map of China areas of growth.
- Name strengths and dangers of this growth pattern for China's development.

Notice that the steps in this learning task are indeed open questions, and that they move across cognitive, affective, and psychomotor aspects of learning.

Implementation Challenge 7A: Face-to-Face

Consider a course you are now teaching or designing for a face-to-face situation. How do you see using your understanding about serial, patterned, and quantum learning? How can this knowledge enhance your design?

Implementation Challenge 7B: On-Line

Consider an on-line course you have designed or taught or are teaching, or one that you have taken. How would changing closed questions to open questions affect that design? Where in that course do you see serial, patterned, and quantum learning?

8

THE DESIGNER'S SKILL

Trust Your Design

A design is like a lectern: you can lean on it!

Once you have done due diligence in preparing your seven step design, it is vital that you trust it to work to enhance learning and make your teaching accountable. Many of us find it tempting to tell learners about what they are trying to learn, rather than to do our duty and teach accountably using dialogue education. The design protects us from that temptation. Follow that design assiduously; lean on it, knowing you can trust it to help learners learn.

Our job is to prepare thoroughly, sensibly, and sensitively, listening to learners through the LNRA, putting the content into a reasonable sequence, building in reinforcement, and setting learners to work. Trust the verbs you have chosen to make learning tasks fruitful.

Clarify the learning task by asking "Is the task clear?" Watch the small group get to work, or not. Where you see confusion in a group, clarify with them specifically. Each time I set a learning task, it is a test—not a test of the learners' knowledge, but a test of my ability to set a clear, substantive, fruitful learning task. When the learning task is clear, you will hear a silence and a buzz of energy in the room as folks get to work: reading, selecting, designing, deciding together, analyzing, synthesizing, building, reviewing—whatever the verb prescribes.

Your design of learning tasks uses the four I's as a resource: inductive, input, implementation, and integration. If it is an inductive learning task, making connections to their life and context, there is a sibilant whisper or hum of sharing in small groups as they *anchor* the upcoming new content. An input learning task gives rise to engaged listening or penciled reading or rapt attention to an attractive outline of content on a PowerPoint slide, as learners find content *added*. The implementation learning task, inviting them to *apply* what they have just read or heard or seen, gets noisy. Small groups get to work on the content, arguing meaning, questioning, critiquing, visualizing, and testing these new ideas or skills in their life and context. It was at this point in a learning task at the University of North Carolina at Chapel Hill when the head of the Department of Health Education at the School of Public Health came into my class and asked: "Jane, why are they always so excited?" Finally, the integration learning task, in which the small group is challenged to take the learning *away*—back home to their context—produces a more reflective, quiet response. Here the creative imagination is at work: *What will it look like when I use this new skill? What does this new theory do to my present relationships?* Because the new theory and new skills have been learned in such a way that the learner has constructed them for herself through the learning tasks in the design, such integration is possible.

It is customary to invite learners to share in the large group after each small-group learning task of each type: inductive, input, implementation, and integration. Even the sharing for each different type is distinctive from the rest. The sample shared from the first inductive task is often tentative and personal. The sample synthesizing input is reflective and thoughtful. The sample of the implementation task gets more energetic and daring: they have put the new content to work and this is what they got. They want to share it! Finally, the sample shared after the integration learning task is quiet again, hopeful, and a bit timid. They are asking: *How will this work in my context?*

Such sharing is a form of reinforcement as well as an extension of learning from one small group to another, from one person to another. Often I see learners nodding assent to what they hear. Sometimes a novel application or hope for integration evokes "Hmm, I never thought of that!" And you can see the interest and excitement on learners' faces.

The Potential of Affirmation

During the learners' sharing of a sample of the products of the learning task, the teacher has an occasion to affirm their work and to add his or her insight on the new content. Here is another temptation I personally face: I am wont to overshadow the learning of students and show how much I know about the new theory or how facile I am in this skill. I want to display my erudition and depth of knowledge and skillfulness. If I stay with the design, I can indeed add to their sample but I must be careful not to overwhelm it. I can connect their contributions and affirm them and show how their insights mesh with mine, or not. I can follow their learning and thus lead them into more learning. A learning task is not about me; it is about learning.

Lavish affirmation of learners' efforts has great potential. It must always be authentic, of course. I can respond to the research of a small group: "That's good work! The depth of what you say indicates you all must have been listening to one another." I can offer application possibilities, anticipating the next part of the learning task: "What you say is still disputed on many levels of this science; in our next task we will get a chance to test it for ourselves." I can affirm inclusion by responding to the thought of a small group: "I can hear a lot of different voices in what you say. Well done!"

Affirmation is not an end in itself: it is a feedback tool that nourishes curiosity, effort, and achievement. Dialogue education is built on learning tasks, which demand feedback and affirmation. I have seen clear evidence of awakening consciousness and confidence after a few words of lavish affirmation in a dialogue education course. When such responses occur, I wonder whether this man or woman has ever heard such words of affirmation before. Charlotte Shelton (1999) speaks to this:

> As we focus on positive aspects, our heart's electromagnetic waves become coherent and the brain's waves spontaneously follow (physicists call this entrainment). From this more coherent state of mind, we see opportunities that we would have missed had we remained stuck in negativity. The opportunities would have been there all along; our emotionally-induced cognitive incoherence simply made them perceptually unavailable to us. Until each of us learns how to create high-energy lives, organizational change programs will make no real difference in either productivity or job satisfaction. Workplace redesign efforts and empowerment processes are necessary but not sufficient. It's the new-wine-in-old-wineskins phenomenon or, in more contemporary language, the second-marriage-same-spouse syndrome. Without an internal shift in consciousness and a new set of emotional choice skills, we keep re-creating the old patterns in our lives, regardless of the new opportunities available to us [p. 8].

Lavish affirmation is intrinsic to the design of dialogue education; it is a way to the internal shift in consciousness and a new set of emotional choice skills that Shelton describes. It is essential to learning.

The Design and Time

Your design has been prepared for a particular time frame. Your job as teacher is to manage that time—set tasks in order and at a brisk pace, time learners' work in the small groups and invite sharing in the large group, synthesize and end a learning task. As I've said, I find using actual clock time a way of fine-tuning the learning task. "We will share your results at 11:10" instead of "I'll give you twenty minutes to complete this task." We do *not* give people time; we can, as managers of the learning situation, set times for particular tasks—for example, sharing in the large group.

Instead of setting times for each learning task, try to work with the whole time frame. In a three-hour period of work, plan to complete five learning tasks with a group of twenty adults. Make that clear to the group. Putting specific times next to a learning task rarely works. So instead of micromanaging time, try to macromanage: set yourself the disciplined task of starting and completing five half-hour learning tasks in three hours. This is a discipline, and again, it keeps us all from the temptation mentioned earlier—to talk about the content in lieu of teaching it.

Design Materials

When possible, have everyone get a copy of the whole seven step design: including all of the learning tasks and relevant materials.

Such a decision evens the playing field. We all know what is expected: *What for?* (the ABOs) and the *What?* (content knowledge, skills, attitudes being taught). Review the complete design in your introduction to a course, and at each session review the specific, related *What?* and *What for?*

It helps to have the learning task either on a flip chart for all to see or projected on a PowerPoint slide. This avoids the confusing note of *What is it we are supposed to be doing?* Such supportive material is not essential, but it is helpful not only to the learners but also to us teachers. Read aloud exactly what the learning task says. When we paraphrase or explain a learning task instead of reading the learning task that everyone has in their materials or on the projector screen, we begin to slide on that slippery slope of temptation: we are en route to telling learners about the content. Telling about is not teaching.

Read what the learning task says! Then ask, "Is the task clear?" Then name the end time when all will share in the large group. Often learners will have entered into the learning task as a small group before you have finished talking. Here's the time for you to sit still, keep quiet, and pay attention.

All About Mnemonics

The printed learning design that each student has, and the learning materials, are valuable memory aids or mnemonics, helping learners remember what the event was all about, what they learned together, and with whom. At the end of a session, those designs and learning materials are often covered with the learner's writing, as each puts his or her own marks on them and takes possession of them.

Global Learning Partners' materials for the course *Learning to Listen, Learning to Teach* include a set of fifty principles and practices designed as a Rolodex, and the seven design steps designed as a set of three-by-five-inch cards. These are valuable mnemonics whose usefulness is manifested by the daily use they get.

These materials are aesthetically pleasing. I find that important as a sign of respect both for the learners and for the highly esteemed content being taught.

The Point of Power

In face-to-face teaching and in on-line sessions, PowerPoint is used to present or illustrate content. I propose that this can be another form of "telling" if it is not used with the intention of transformational learning via dialogue education. We can use a one-quarter approach to make the PowerPoint instrument a servant to learning: make the PowerPoint materials one-quarter of the learning session and design an input task around the PowerPoint presentation.

Resistance

Initially, a dialogue education design can receive strong resistance from organizers of educational events and from learners. Trust your design. You have spent hours preparing this and deserve at least the same respect that you give the learners.

Example

I was preparing a design for a short course for professors at a university medical school in North Carolina, and, as is my custom,

I shared the design with the course organizer, whose response was horror mixed with terror mixed with anger. *"Never!"* I recall her saying. *"Never! You can never ask physicians to talk to one another during a class."*

I smiled and made the adjustments necessary to get the course started. In fact, the physicians did talk to one another and learned from that dialogue. I understood the resistance of the organizer, who was accountable to a number of hierarchies. Trust your design—but do not thrust your design at people who are not prepared for it.

Learners will often complain and demand, *Just tell us the facts, and let us go home.* Happily, in most circumstances the teacher can design a class or a session or a course according to her best lights. Trust your design in the face of such complaints. We can never justify the process; rather, we can get on with the process, which justifies itself in its fruitfulness. Learners' resistance is rarely long-lived. In spite of themselves, they get caught up in a good, tough learning task.

No Polemic Here

To be congruent with the principles and practices of dialogue education and to effect transformational learning, we cannot make this educational approach a polemic. Dialogue cannot be preached. Some situations demand our giving up the forms of dialogue to implement true dialogue, which is a frame of mind through which we listen to others.

The following story, a personal memory, describes such a situation, which ended well, thanks to the courage of a determined physician. As we well know, other situations, in which resistance prevails, end less happily.

Resistance Overcome by Courage

At the United Nations in New York in 1991, a number of leading physicians from around the world had been invited to a conference on designing AIDS training. The Indian physician in charge of coordinating the conference, Dr. A., had hired me to design with a core team. The night before the conference was to start, a small group of doctors came to her complaining that the program they had received did not follow the usual conference protocols: learned speeches given from a podium by learned physicians and researchers. Dr. A. relented, and she told me she planned to restructure the conference. She invited me to stay overnight and attend the first day.

I was saddened by her decision, although I understood the pressure she felt. At about ten that evening, the phone rang in my hotel room. It was Dr. A. "Please consider leading the conference according to our original plan," she said. "I realize that the dialogue approach is imperative here."

The next morning we began the conference with Dr. A. introducing the process and me as the leader. I set the first learning task for the group, who were somewhat reluctant to get started. One of the members of the core team (Dr. T.), who had been most outspoken in his opposition to a dialogue education format, sat almost sullenly at his group's table. He was a well-dressed European physician, wearing an expensive suit and tie, highly shined shoes, and a grim visage. I watched him as the group set to work on the first learning task, inviting inductive reflection on the scope of the problem in their unique contexts. After a few moments, his expensive jacket came off and was draped over the back of his chair. Then I saw him open his shirt collar and loosen his tie. The dialogue was heating up. Soon Dr. T. was in the midst of it, and the fur was flying. Learning was going on apace, and there was not an expert at a lectern in sight. They were, of course, all experts, sharing not only their ideas but also their passion and their power.

Across the room, I saw Dr. A. watching the learning groups; when I caught her eye, she smiled and mouthed a silent "Thank you." She had trusted the design, and it was bearing fruit in learning for all. I wish we had had at that time the tools for evaluation (see Chapter Nine) that we have now: how useful it would be to know what learning took place in that room and what transfer and impact followed the conference!

Frame the Learning Task

When you are faithful to your design, you place it in a frame that enhances the learning potential of everyone in the room. The frame is the overall design, with content specified and objectives clearly set forth. The time frame is nonnegotiable, so the teacher is accountable to do all of the learning tasks in the overall design within that time frame. Learning is not arbitrary, dependent on the attentiveness or intelligence of the learner. The event is not a brilliant performance by a sagacious and learned teacher. It is a faithful design for learning.

Each learning task follows on the previous one in an explicit and clear sequence, so the frame itself is evident. As learners work each task, they naturally make reference to preceding learning tasks and new knowledge and skills already gained. The skillful dialogue educator celebrates each reference, thus reinforcing the continuous learning. The frame extends and opens to embrace contiguous interests of learners—but there is always a frame.

A Broken Frame

When I was in high school, I led my classmates in a seditious effort to break the frame in the classroom of a particular old nun who was given to philosophizing. One or the other of us was set each day to ask a broad, irrelevant question quite apart from the topic at hand. Once we had hooked the teacher by this question, we could sit back and be entertained by her musings and memories. I confess this at this late date to show how easy it is to break the frame and get a leader to abandon his design.

Trust Your Design

Do not leave the design except to implement a new one that you have made. Dialogue education happens best by design. Such design is always intentional. In our next section we will examine how we can evaluate the effectiveness of such intentional design.

Design On-Line

As we have already seen, the structure of an on-line course, its design, is operative throughout. All that has been said so far about fidelity to that design applies on-line. Making the design accessible and transparent is the responsibility of the course designer. I was impressed and inspired by the careful design work that went into the on-line course I recently took at University of Detroit Mercy. When the whole world is your market, the quality of your educational product is vital.

Implementation Challenge 8A: Face-to-Face

Consider a situation in which you are teaching a professional course and you discover that your design offers too much *What?* for the *When?* You realize that there is no way you will complete the syllabus in the given time frame. You must make changes to the design. Consider one way you will go about that in the light of all that this chapter has offered.

Implementation Challenge 8B: On-Line

Consider this situation: you are leading an on-line course that you have designed. This is the first run of your course. It becomes clear in week two that some of the directions are ambiguous and confusing to on-line learners, especially those for whom English is not their first language. What do you see as your options, in light of what you have read so far in this book?

Part Four

SURE

How do they know they know? They just did it.

9

INDICATORS OF LEARNING, TRANSFER, AND IMPACT

Learning is what occurs within the event, *transfer*
is taking that learning to a new context, and *impact* is
the change in organizations and systems caused by
that learning.

Outcomes, results, success—these words reign in the world of
education today. A consumer society insists on getting what they
have paid for through taxes or fees. One way to consider effects of
teaching is to identify indicators—of learning, of transfer of learning to the learner's context, and of impact on the society or organization. In this dialogue education framework, we can be guided
by the *What for?* of the seven design steps, which shows us our
achievement-based objectives (ABOs). These can lead to identifi-
cation of specific indicators of learning.

Learning, Transfer, Impact

In our 1997 book *How Do They Know They Know?* my colleagues
Paula Berardinelli and Jim Burrow and I shared research on the
threefold measures of results: learning, transfer, and impact. We
suggest that behavioral learning indicators can be seen within
the learning event; transfer indicators are visible as learners use
new knowledge and skills in their own context, at work, at home,
in their community; and impact indicators show changes in the
behavior of systems or organizations as a result of learning and
transfer. In this chapter we will show the relationship of learning

to transfer and to impact, and how indicators of each can be identified and documented.

Learning

Learning is what takes place in a session as a result of intentional teaching. The seven design steps lay out definitively the content of a session: the set of nouns that show exactly what learners will work with to learn. For example, I teach the twelve basic principles and practices of dialogue education. You use these explicitly in creating a design, speak of them as you analyze that design and review your teaching practice, and add dimensions to some of them from your own context. This behavior of yours and the corollary products are indicators of learning.

We know that we cannot determine what people will learn in a session. We also know the quantum principle: a holistic perspective tells us that the whole is greater than the sum of its parts. We know learners often learn more than our design tries to teach. However, it is our duty to say what indicators of learning we expect and to design the session to achieve those indicators. We are accountable. The seven design steps do that implicitly by naming a discrete set of content (*What?*), stating ABOs (*What for?*), and laying out learning tasks (*How?*) that make them happen. In a well-designed learning task we can begin to see behavioral products emerge that are indicators of learning.

For example, in an adult education course teaching the four parts of a learning task—inductive work (anchoring the new learning in the life and context of the learners), input (adding new content), implementation (applying the content), and integration (taking the content away back home)—we name the content (*What?*). The learning task for this has a clear title (*How?*) and four parts.

Learning Task: Four Elements in a Learning Task

A learning task is an open question put to a small group, with all the materials they need to respond. A learning task is a task for the learner.

1. In pairs, review one of the learning tasks we have done in this course so far. What do you notice about them? Tell one another how such learning tasks might inform your work.

2. Read this chart:

   Learning tasks often have four elements:
   a. Inductive work (anchoring the new learning in the life and context of the learners)
   b. Input (adding new content)
   c. Implementation (applying the content)
   d. Integration (taking the content away, back home)

3. Examine the learning tasks in this course to discover any one of these four elements. We'll hear a sample. What are your questions about these elements?

4. In pairs, select a topic you are soon going to teach. Sketch a learning task, using all four elements if they are appropriate to your topic. Put your learning task in four parts on the wall on a sheet of flip chart paper for all to see.

As small groups grapple with the learning tasks, they are engaged, working in supportive teams, offering one another safety, affirmation, respect, and a challenge.

As they move through these four elements, they define them for themselves and construct this theory in such a way that it will be useful to them in their context. There is no pure theory here, nothing to be defended or affirmed. Theory is always waiting to be tested, disproved, changed, improved, developed.

Each small group's learning task, related to a specific content piece from their context, can be celebrated as a unique representation of the theory at work and in evolution. The affirmation offered by the teacher is not for a right answer, but for a solid piece of work.

Notice that there is an indicator of learning in the response to learning task 4—the integrative element of the learning task—and in the response to learning task 3 as well, in which learners discover these elements and then question both them and the theory. We begin to see behavioral products that are indeed indicators of learning.

Other Indicators of Learning

Behaviors manifesting learning can emerge right from the learning task, as in the example given. They can also be more informal: the language used and understood by the group, individual gestures and body language, facility in basic skills that are called for in more difficult learning tasks, planning for use of content in their context, changing of designs or lesson plans to incorporate new content, sharing of news about skills and content with colleagues. In a graduate school or college setting, they can also be more formal: planning within a course to use new skills and content in subsequent papers and projects. In any case, they are behaviors manifesting the learning that has just taken place.

It is often exhilarating for members of a class or course to identify and discover indicators of learning. Because they have already read the seven design steps and know what we set as ABOs (*What for?*), they are primed to name these indicators as they see them emerge from themselves or their colleagues. In a recent short course, a nurse educator in a small group was heard talking about how she was already designing the LNRA for her upcoming course for mothers. The others in the group celebrated an indicator of learning in her behavior. In the introductory course offered by Global Learning Partners, *Learning to Listen, Learning to Teach*, teams design and teach twice and receive feedback on their performance and on their design. In both the first and second teaching practice, they can see indicators of learning in their various behaviors: how they design, how they work together, what they decide in terms of principles, how they speak to the "learners," how they even accept suggestions for improvement. We as teachers are responsible to catch every indicator and affirm it. We quantify and celebrate their learning. In turn, they can celebrate our teaching.

Current evaluation language speaks of *outcomes*. In one sense, these behaviors manifesting learning are immediate outcomes, designated and designed for by our seven design steps.

Transfer

The transfer of learning is measured by behavior that takes place after the course or seminar or training session. Men and women get back to their workplace or community or home and begin to do what they learned: putting concepts into action and practicing new skills. These actions are indicators of transfer and can be documented and measured.

For example, an adult learner takes an on-line course on the form and function of the brain. After the month-long course, she describes her learning to her family and shares with them her decision to purchase only whole-grain breads, changing her family's nutritional pattern. That is an indicator of transfer. She begins to play the piano, after years of neglect, to stimulate a particular part of her brain. That is transfer. She continues her study of this topic by enrolling in a second course in the sequence. She reads a number of books on the brain that are suggested in the curriculum. These are further indicators of transfer.

Notice that transfer is sometimes direct: you do at home or at work exactly what you practiced doing in the learning session. It is sometimes indirect: you integrate the new concepts and skills gently into your general behavior. You eat more fruits and vegetables and exercise more regularly because you know exactly what effect these practices have on your brain.

Behaviors manifesting transfer of learning might be called *longitudinal outcomes*. Often such behaviors occur within the time frame of a five-day course. Language changes, the sequence of actions is intentional, collaboration is enhanced: these are recognized by learners as transfer indicators.

The Eighth Design Step. I see an awareness of transfer as a design step that can be added to our seven design steps: perhaps we can call it *So What?* We set up ABOs saying, *By the end of this session, all will have . . .* using tough, specific verbs to ensure learning. If we were to design an eighth design step, we might say, *By the end of the week after this course, all participants will have . . .* and anticipate transfer. For example, after the *Learning to Listen, Learning to Teach* course, which teaches the basic principles and practices of dialogue education, we might say in the eighth design step: *By the end of the week after this course, all participants will have*

- Begun to redesign their present courses using the seven design steps
- Designed an LNRA for an upcoming course
- Used learning tasks in a staff meeting
- Sent new designs for review by the course leader

This would not be incongruent with our understanding of transfer. It would be indicative of the trust we have in the design, in our skills and in our passion, in their learning and their ability to take that learning home.

Asking for Indicators of Transfer. We can formalize a system of requests for indicators of transfer. I usually tell clients that I will call them a month after the educational event or consultation to invite descriptions of indicators of transfer. I tell them I welcome e-mail from them with specific indicators relevant to their situation. This is the only way we can assure clients that we are accountable. Without specific, explicit indicators of transfer, a training program or a course has not been accountable.

A Research Agenda. All who study and use dialogue education have the responsibility to work on the ongoing outcomes research agenda, which will document baseline situations and show training designs and products, with indicators of learning and accrued indicators of transfer (outcomes).

Indicators and Outcomes. Learning is often manifested in behavior. This concern for transfer will please educators who use outcome-based education or results-based education. All that they are asking for is accountability within the educational design and process. Transfer indicators are results, sometimes called outcomes, based on the careful design of the content (*What?*) and the ABOs (*What for?*) in the course. These in turn are based on a sound reading of the group being taught (*Who?*) and the situation that calls for the learning (*Why?*).

Again, as we learn in quantum thinking, the whole is more than the sum of its parts. Men and women are going to learn more than we teach. They are going to reconstruct the theory and skills we teach to fit their lives and context. The test of our success is their immediate, useful transfer. So what? New skills, new theories, new behaviors are in place in their old workplace, in their community, and in their homes, and they begin to see signs of health. From transfer to impact is often a long, step-by-step journey of single steps marked by indicators. We make the way by walking, indeed.

Impact

Changes in organizational structure or systems as a function of an educational event are indicators of impact. The American Society for the Prevention of Cruelty to Animals (ASPCA), for example, now teaches dialogue education to all of their staff. They have come to realize that in all of their interventions with pet owners, they are doing adult education. This is a major systems change. Further impact indicators can be documented as ASPCA's clients are more competently served and share their satisfaction.

Habitat for Humanity and Freedom from Hunger are two other organizations that have made dialogue education an integral part of their culture.

Impact is the end of the affair, the purpose of your teaching. Impact is sometimes specific as particular systems change; however, it is often general: a new state of mind, a new attitude, or a renewed sense of original purpose. You as educator or trainer may never know the details of the impact your work achieved. But each tiny movement towards enhanced, responsible learning, towards peacefulness and self-respect, represents the impact of your work. We will further examine impact indicators in the next chapter.

Implementation Challenge 9A: Face-to-Face

Consider a course you have taken or taught. Name one specific indicator of learning and one specific indicator of transfer from that course.

Implementation Challenge 9B: On-Line

Consider the systems changes we are seeing as a function of on-line learning. What impact can you imagine for on-line courses when they use dialogue education? If you were designing an on-line course, what one aspect of what you have read so far in this book would you use?

10

IMPACT AND THE SEVEN DESIGN STEPS

The quality of education impacts the quality of life.

In 1991 Paula Berardinelli presented a theory of impact that has deeply influenced how dialogue education looks at evaluation. She suggests that we can name indicators of learning (what occurs during the session), indicators of transfer (what learners take home), and indicators of *impact* (the qualitative and quantitative differences in people and organizations as the result of the educational event).

Impact is long-range, of course. When I was a teacher at a girls' high school in Tanzania in the 1960s and 1970s, we would say, "When these young women are grandmothers, we will see the impact of our work." Managers of organizations set up training sessions and educational programs for impact, often confusing this with transfer. Berardinelli showed us how important it is to recognize this difference. Impact is what happens to an organization, a family, a church, a company, a nation as a result of an educational venture.

Impact indicators are directly related to the *Why?* question of the seven design steps. The *Why?* step (the situation that calls for this educational event) spells out what the *Who?* (participants) need. Here is an example to clarify this connection:

Example

Course Title: Parents' Education: How to Talk with Your Kids about Drinking

Who? A chapter of the PTA of Moore County School (thirty parents) They have all read *Family Talk: How to Talk With Your Kids*

About Drinking: A Guide for Parents (Anheuser-Busch, 2005 [www .familytalkonline.com]) and marked up their copies in preparation for this course.

Why? These parents are concerned about the threat of drinking that their children face. They need to know how to talk to their children and what they can tell them to ensure that their children do not drink until they are twenty-one. They need to prevent the scourge of DUI (driving under the influence) and traffic accidents and other problems in families and in the community caused by drinking.

When? Three two-hour sessions: Monday evenings for three weeks

Where? The school hall, a room with tables for group work

What? These six guidelines from the Anheuser-Busch booklet *Family Talk:*

1. Be a good role model.
2. Be factual.
3. Have clearly stated rules.
4. Practice good parenting.
5. Know your children's friends and their parents.
6. Get help if you need it.

What for? By the end of this series of three two-hour sessions, all will have

- Read Family Talk: How to Talk With Your Kids About Drinking: A Guide for Parents (Anheuser-Busch, 2005)
- Named ways parents can be good role models for their children (Guideline 1)
- Practiced a family conversation about responsible adult drinking (Guideline 1)
- Identified facts about the effects of alcohol (Guideline 2)

- Considered "the teachable years—nine to eleven" (Guideline 3)
- Related particular problems faced in the teen years (Guideline 3)
- Practiced setting clearly stated rules (Guideline 3)
- Named ways to practice good parenting in their own setting (Guideline 4)
- Listed their children's friends and their parents' names (Guideline 5)
- Practiced talking to a teen about using ways to say "No" (Guideline 5)
- Identified resources they know or can use (Guideline 6)
- Named signs of trouble that might call for access to outside resources (Guideline 6)
- Described preferred family strategies for working with teens (Guideline 6)
- Reviewed a case study of a teen arrested for DUI (Guideline 6)

How? Learning tasks and materials

Learning Task 1: Family Talk: A Guide for Parents
1A. You have read and marked up the booklet. At your table, tell what you have marked or underlined. We'll hear a sample.

1B. Identify friends or relatives whom you think could use this booklet. List these to give to the course leader. At your table, describe one thing you would tell these friends about the booklet. We'll hear a sample.

Learning Task 2: Being Good Role Models
2A. At your table, reflect on one thing your parents did to be good role models as you were growing up. What do you notice about the examples offered? We'll hear a sample.

2B. Name one thing you do to be a good role model that you are proud of. We'll share a sample.

2C. Write on a card one thing you want to do differently. Put the card in your purse or wallet. Later, at home, talk with your spouse about what you wrote.

Learning Task 3: Family Conversations

3A. At your table, select one of the conversations on pages 46–51 of *Family Talk*. Take parts and read the conversation aloud. Name one way you would change it at your home.

3B. Select another conversation. Take parts and read the conversation aloud. Name one way you would change it at your home.

Learning Task 4: The Effects of Alcohol

4A. List on sticky notes what you know of the immediate effects of drinking alcohol. Review page 15.

4B. In pairs, name ways you can share these facts with your own children.

4C. Describe at your table how you might speak to your son as he begins driving lessons. What one idea at your table was compelling? We'll hear all.

Learning Task 5: Nine to Eleven

What does the note "The best years to talk about drinking with your children are nine to eleven" say to you? Share with your partner. We'll hear a sample.

Learning Task 6: The Teen Years

6A. In new pairs, tell one story from your own teen years. Name what this tells you about teens.

6B. Describe at your table how you might speak to your son or daughter as he or she begins driving lessons. What one idea at your table was compelling? We'll hear all.

Learning Task 7: Clearly Stated Rules

List some necessary rules about drinking you want your family to follow. Share these at your table. Look at the final list. What would you add?

Learning Task 8: Practice Good Parenting

8A. In new pairs, describe how you try to create an atmosphere of open communication. Share your strategies at the table. We'll hear a sample.

8B. In pairs, describe a recent family activity that was a healthy, happy time. Name one new activity you might want to try in future. We'll hear a sample.

Learning Task 9: Friends and Their Parents

9A. Each write a list of your children's friends, one page for each child.

9B. Write their friends' parents' names and phone numbers if you know them. In pairs, tell your partner what you want to do with this list.

Learning Task 10: Saying No

10A. Each pair at each table write a situation in which a teenager will have to say "No, thanks" to friends who are about to drink and drive. Take one of the situations and as a pair, decide how you will speak to your sons or daughters about it (see pages 35–36 of *Family Talk*).

10B. At your table, tell what you would add to these strategies on page 40.

Learning Task 11: Identified Resources That Can Help

At your table, tell what you know about the resources named on page 38 of *Family Talk*. Tell what resources you would add to this list. We'll hear all your additions.

Learning Task 12: Signs of Trouble

At your table, read through the list of signs of trouble in a teen (page 39 of *Family Talk*). Decide what you would add to this list. We'll hear all.

Learning Task 13: Preferred Family Strategies for Working with Teens

In new pairs, read over the strategies on page 40 of *Family Talk*. Describe what you would add to this list. We'll hear all your additions.

Learning Task 14: A Case Study of a Teen Arrested for DUI

14A. Read aloud at your table the steps on pages 42–43 of *Family Talk*, putting the name on your table into the place of "the teen."

14B. In pairs, share what you might be feeling, were you the parent of that child. Name one thing you have learned in this series that will prevent that event for you and your family.

———————

Notice that in their actual working through the learning tasks, parents are demonstrating their *learning* of the content: the six guidelines. Those learning tasks that involve projection invite indicators of potential *transfer*. What can you anticipate as the *impact* of this simple course on the parents, their children, the community, the school? Here are some possibilities:

• Decrease in the number of youth who admit to drinking

• Decrease in the number of teen fatalities from drunk driving accidents (from police reports)

• Decrease in the number of DUI arrests (from police reports)

• Increase in the number of students in sports programs (from school reports)

- A decrease in sales of alcoholic drinks at shops near the schools
- Lower number of children sent to rehab centers(from DCF reports)
- Fewer children attending the community clinic (from clinic reports)
- Improved rates of acceptance into college and university (from school reports)

Measuring Impact. School administrators who set up dialogue education courses using the materials described here can do research studies to establish a baseline for this quantitative evaluation before the courses begin. All of these indicators can be measured for present baseline status at the beginning of the series. What other impact indicators for this particular program for parents might you name?

Impact studies are done over time; however, publication of early data can be encouraging to parents, the community, and the course organizers and leaders. Qualitative aspects of impact—such as more peaceful homes, less sibling arguing and tension, more family time spent together, increased laughter in families—are more difficult to determine from a baseline, but no less important in the life of a community. What other qualitative indicators might work for this educational endeavor with families?

Examine again the situation that calls for this educational event:

> Why? (the situation): These parents are concerned about the threat of drinking that their children face. They need to know how to talk to their children and what they can tell them to ensure that their children do not drink until they are twenty-one. They need to prevent the scourge of DUI and traffic accidents and other problems in families and in the community caused by drinking.

Course organizers, community leaders, teachers, parents, clergy, medical personnel, and the children themselves are all involved. As soon as the course series begins, learning indicators and transfer indicators can be seen. The purpose of this educational endeavor however, is *impact*. Berardinelli's discovery is the theory of *impact*. Dialogue education is accountable for such impact. We are accountable for learning and transfer, yes, but these are not enough. What is the *impact* of our educational work, and how can we accountably measure it?

Sample Impact Measurement Matrix. N = number of teen age children of all parents involved in the courses

The IMM is a simple instrument offering baseline data and annual figures on each item over a period of five years.

Baseline Data

- Number of students in cohort who admit to drinking in this calendar year
- Number of teen fatalities from drunk driving accidents (from local police reports in this calendar year)
- Number of DUI arrests among age cohort in this calendar year (from local police reports)
- Number of students in sports programs from school reports for this calendar year
- Sales of alcoholic drinks at shops near the schools for this calendar year (survey)
- Number of children sent to rehab centers this calendar year (from local DCF reports)
- Number of children attending the community clinic (from local clinic reports)
- Rates of acceptance into college and university among the cohort age group (from school reports)
- What other baseline data would serve?

Hard Work of Preparation

Designing a course from excellent materials as dialogue education, using the seven design steps, means hard work and time spent doing it. Whatever you are teaching—parents' education about drinking, nutrition, college courses in any discipline, church courses on the Millennium Development Goals—you are teaching for learning that makes a difference in a person's life. That is *impact*. Measuring impact begins with the seven design steps. Research begins with the following:

> *Who?* (participants): Who are the folks who need this most? Who can do the most with this new knowledge, or new skills or attitudes?

It continues with the crucial

> *Why?* (the situation): What is the real-life situation that demands this learning and transfer?

These two central questions control your decision about what is to be included in the content and how the ABOs and the learning tasks are framed.

Designing an appropriate impact measurement matrix (IMM) means hard work and time spent doing it *before the course begins*. Current quantitative baseline data on projected, named impact indicators is essential to the credibility of the endeavor.

It has been my personal experience that projected impact indicators named at the outset of a course grow and develop into something beyond the projection by virtue of the learning and transfer that take place within and after the course.

Impact is a measurement of success, and success is contagious. The hard, detailed work needed in the design of both course work and an IMM with all the necessary baseline data seems overwhelming. It is hard and demanding until you do it—and discover how such structures evoke spontaneity and creativity in all involved. Learning and transfer are the yeast that bubble up in the stirred and kneaded dough and lead to the fragrant, nourishing bread of *impact*.

Implementation Challenge 10A: Face-to-Face

Consider a course you have recently designed and taught. Describe what you might have done to connect the seven design steps to the indicators of *learning*, *transfer*, and *impact*. Sketch an IMM with baseline data that you could have used.

Name the advantage to you and your organization of such work. In chapters Thirteen, Fourteen, and Fifteen you will see the overt connection between the seven design steps and indicators of *learning*, *transfer*, and *impact*.

Implementation Challenge 10B: Online

Decide where you would put the IMM for an online course—at the beginning with the instructions to students, or later?

Decide how you can get the necessary baseline research done. How can you involve on-line learners in the completion of that research? In Chapter Twelve you will find an example of a dialogue education design for an on-line course in which learners are involved in building the IMM.

Part Five

SYNTHESIS: PUTTING IT ALL TOGETHER

The whole is more than the sum of its parts.

11

PUTTING IT ALL TOGETHER

Examples of Dialogue Education Designs

This chapter first presents a short course that introduces dialogue education through four protocols that newcomers may practice until they have occasion to take the course *Learning to Listen, Learning to Teach* (www.globalearning.com). As you review this design, look for the use of all of the principles and practices named in the book so far: the seven design steps and the LNRA; learning tasks with their four component parts; and indicators of learning, transfer, and impact.

Then we examine the design for a short course on dialogue education that was offered to faculty and graduate students at Simon Frasier University in Vancouver, British Columbia, Canada. A third example comes from the annual Medical Education Conference offered each year in Philadelphia. The final example in this chapter is a single session on the four parts of a learning task from Global Learning Partners' Advanced Design Course.

Tate Museum, London: Four Protocols for Effective Learning

This course was offered in London, England at the Tate Museum in May 2006 to introduce dialogue education and Global Learning Partners, Inc. to European educators. Sophie Howarth, a curator at the Tate involved in community education, had come to Raleigh, North Carolina to take the introductory course in dialogue education. She was so impressed with her success using this to design and teach that she organized a short seminar for educators in the London and other parts of the UK. Here is the seven step design that was provided to participants:

Dialogue Education Seminar: The Seven Design Steps

Who? (The participants, leaders)

Up to one hundred participants who are educators in the UK. All of the participants are involved in organizing, designing, or facilitating different learning events. They have different levels of experience and familiarity with dialogue education. These include the ten who have just completed the *Learning to Listen, Learning to Teach* course with Karen Ridout.

Participants have registered for the seminar. They have been invited to offer their response via e-mail to a simple learning needs and resources assessment (LNRA) survey.

Global Learning Partners (www.globalearning.com) assists individuals and organizations to apply the principles and practices of dialogue education to enhance the process and results of their educational efforts.

Dr. Jane Vella, founder of GLP, and GLP senior associate and partner Karen Ridout will lead the seminar.

Why? (The situation that calls for the event)

Dr. Jane Vella is taking this opportunity to demonstrate the value of dialogue education to educators in the UK. She and her colleague Karen Ridout will provide an overview of dialogue education. After the seminar, an informal session will provide time for ongoing dialogue.

When? (The time)

May 12, 2006: three hours.

Where? (The location)

A large space with movable tables and chairs to accommodate up to one hundred participants and two leaders. An LCD projector and screen, a flip chart, and available wall space will be used.

What? (The content)

What is dialogue education? How does it enhance adult learning? Four protocols to begin the use of dialogue education:

1. The seven design steps and the LNRA
2. Learning tasks—four elements:
   - Inductive work to anchor the new content
   - Input: add new content
   - Implementation: Learners apply new ideas or skills
   - Integration: Learners take it away
3. Selected principles and practices
4. Evaluation indicators: learning, transfer, impact

This seminar will use dialogue education throughout.

What for? (Achievement-based objectives)

By the end of this three-hour seminar, all participants will have

- Experienced dialogue education, using learning tasks.
- Examined twelve principles and practices of dialogue education.
- Considered how the LNRA enables the dialogue to begin before the event and considered using an LNRA for their context.
- Reviewed the seven design steps and named ways this might work in their context.
- Defined a learning task and examined the four elements of a learning task.

- Reviewed the concepts of learning, transfer and impact.
- Identified resources for continuing study of dialogue education: Global Learning Partners, Inc. (www.globalearning.com).
- Posed questions, invited responses, and continued the dialogue in an informal setting after the seminar.

How? (Learning tasks and materials)

Introduction: What Is Dialogue Education?

Learning Task 1: Some Principles and Practices of Dialogue Education

- Learning needs and resources assessment
- Safety
- Sound relationships
- Sequence and reinforcement
- Praxis
- Respect
- Ideas/feelings/actions
- Immediacy
- Teamwork
- Engagement
- Clear roles
- Accountability

1A. In pairs, with someone you do not know, review the twelve principles and practices that are on your tables. Ask questions about any that are not clear to you, of your colleague or of Jane or Karen.

1B. Tell your colleague how you *already* use at least three of these to achieve quality education.

1C. Name one of these that you see is the hardest to implement in your unique context. We'll hear a sample and suggest ways to deal with the ones named.

Learning Task 2: The Learning Needs and Resources Assessment.
Learning needs and resources assessment *informs* but does not *form*
the program.

   2A. In new pairs, tell how you already do some kind of prepara-
       tory research in your context. We'll hear a sample.

   2B. Look at the questions on the survey you received. Name
       other questions you would have liked to have been asked.
       Introduction to Dialogue Education: Three hours on May
       12, 2006
       Learning Needs and Resources Assessment

       The LNRA is an important strategy of dialogue education,
          beginning the dialogue before the event. Please respond
          to these two questions and send your response to Sophie
          Howarth (sophie.howarth@tate.org.uk) by May 3, 2006.

       1. Describe your present involvement in education.

       2. Describe one educational practice in your situation
          that you are proud of. We work best and grow *from our
          strengths.*

       3. What are your questions about dialogue education?

Learning Task 3: The Seven Design Steps
   3A. In new pairs, examine the seven design steps used for this
       seminar. What are your questions?

   3B. In the same pairs, name one place these seven design steps
       would be useful in your context. We'll hear all.

Learning Task 4: Four Elements of a Learning Task
A learning task is an open question put to a small group, with all
the resources they need to respond.

   4A. We've just done three learning tasks. At your table, name
       what struck you about them.

4B. Listen to an explanation of the four elements of an effective learning task.

Inductive work: Anchor new learning in life

Input: Add new content—substantive, accessible, immediate

Implementation: Do something with that new content—apply it now

Integration: Take it home and away!

4C. Examine, as a table group, the learning tasks we've just completed. Where do you see these elements reflected in those learning tasks, or not? We'll hear a sample of your responses.

Learning Task 5: Evaluation Indicators: Learning, Transfer and Impact (evolution)

5A. Read and mark up the following notes:

Learning relates to the content of the program or project. We look for indicators before people leave a session. Indicators of learning are behavioral.

Transfer is what happens when men and women take that behavior back home or back to the work place the next day. Again, the indicator is a behavior.

Impact (evolution) is the change that takes place in organizations and systems as a function of the transfer and learning. Indicators are changes in the behaviors of these systems.

5B. In new pairs, name some indicators of learning you are *already* seeing in this seminar. We'll hear a sample.

5C. Identify some indicators of transfer we might see on Monday from this short seminar. We'll hear a sample.

5D. Dream a little. What impact might dialogue education, well designed and well implemented, have on your educational context? That is, how might the system or organization *evolve* as a function of this kind of learning? We'll hear a sample.

Indicators of Learning

The Tate Museum event was planned and implemented with all the panache of an English afternoon with the queen. The East Room of the Tate Gallery is a brilliant venue for such learning. Guests were warmly welcomed, the event was videotaped, and small interest groups naturally formed as people discovered colleagues from adult learning centers in Wales, Ireland, and England.

After the brief introduction, small groups got into learning tasks, and it was virtually impossible to draw them back from their intense dialogue at their tables to share in the large group. The noise level in the room was an indicator in itself of excitement and hopeful learning dialogue. At one point a young adult educator from Cardiff stood to offer a synopsis of his group's work and said, very proudly, "I am Ian, and it's Welsh I am."

These adult educators came to learn about dialogue education and stayed to teach it by working together very generously. Afterward, we drank wine and talked into the night, sitting on the balcony of the Tate Restaurant overlooking the Thames and St. Paul's.

My Reflections

Because this seminar was so tightly designed, the three hours were spent in learning. I was prevented from talking about dialogue education. Instead, everyone in the room (even the technicians behind their complex audio and video apparatus) was engaged in learning. There were valuable connections made that afternoon, not with Jane Vella, but with colleagues committed to adult learning from all parts of Great Britain.

When they left that seminar, they could not say how brilliant the presenter was; they could and did exclaim about what they had learned from one another. "Only connect."

Simon Fraser University, Vancouver: Seven Design Steps

This section presents a short course on the use of the seven design steps in planning and organizing a teaching session. This was actually offered at Simon Fraser University in Vancouver, British Columbia, in 2006. Note that we use the seven design steps to design the short course and to teach it.

Designing Education with the Seven Design Steps

Who? (The participants)

From thirty to forty university professors, and the staff of several professional centers based at the university. These men and women come from various disciplines. Some are familiar with dialogue education; some are not.

Why? (The situation that calls for this event)

University professors are anxious for more focused, more lively, and more engaged teaching. Students have asked for this over the years. The Dialogue Centre at the University highlights their search to use dialogue for enhanced learning. They need a system that ensures quality control of teaching and learning.

When? (The time frame)

Two-hour professional development workshop.

Where? (The site)

A pleasant hall equipped with round tables for small-group work.

What? (The content)

The seven design steps

- How to use these in designing your classes.
- Connection between seven steps and learning tasks.

What for? (The achievement-based objectives)

By the end of this two-hour session, all will have:

- Reviewed all seven design steps in sequence.
- Identified the connection between these and learning tasks.
- Practiced designing a class or course with the seven design steps.

How? (The learning tasks and materials)

Learning Task 1: The Seven Design Steps

1A. In pairs, examine the design for this two-hour workshop. Note the steps used and the sequence:

Who? Why?

When? Where?

What? What for?

How?

1B. Decide as a pair which is the most important question or set of questions in the design process, and why. Share your pair's responses at your table. We'll hear a sample.

1C. As a table group, name the reasons you see for this sequence. We'll hear all.

Learning Task 2: Connection Between Seven Steps and Learning Tasks

2A. In new pairs, examine the learning task we just completed. Read this description:

> A learning task is an open question put to a small group, with all the resources they need to respond.

Tell where you see open questions in Learning Task 1.

Tell where you see *the resources needed to respond.* We'll hear all.

2B. At your table, show the connection you see between the learning task and the seven design steps. We'll hear a sample.

Learning Task 3: Practice Designing

3A. In new pairs, each select a situation in which you are preparing a course, seminar, workshop, or single lesson. Give the session a title. Share your titles at your table.

3B. Use the seven design steps to sketch a design for that session. Write at least one content piece (*What?*) and one corollary achievement-based objective (*What for?*) and the learning task (*How?*) for that content and objective. Review one another's designs; share them at your table.

3C. At your table, describe what use you see for these seven design steps in your context. We'll hear all.

Mnemonics and Follow-up

Each participant left the workshop with a set of cards with each of the seven design steps and with a sketch of a design they had created using the seven steps. They were all invited to the follow-up professional development session on learning tasks.

Medical Education Conference, Philadelphia: Learning Needs and Resources Assessment (LNRA)

This is short course on the design and use of the learning needs and resources assessment as an essential aspect of dialogue education. This short course was part of a larger workshop at the Medical Education Conference in Philadelphia in 2006.

Beginning the Dialogue Before the Lesson

Who? (The participants, leader)

Over one hundred medical doctors, nurses, and pharmacists at the annual Medical Education Conference. Conference organizers had heard of dialogue education and were keen on sharing the LNRA concept and practice. Each of the participants was sent an e-mail with an LNRA for this workshop. The response was minimal.

Why? (The situation)

These men and women have come to the conference to discover ways to improve and enhance their medical education practices.

When? (The time frame)

Sixty minutes in a day of six such hour-long workshops.

Where? (The site)

A large hall at a conference center. The audience is seated in rows and the speaker is at a lectern in front of them, with a large screen for projections behind her.

What? (The content)

- What an LNRA is and does.
- Research-based rules of design of an LNRA.
- Research-based effective modes of utilization.

What for? (Achievement-based objectives)

By the end of this hour, all will have:

- Defined a learning needs and resources assessment for their context.
- Examined the rules of design and amended them for their context.
- Selected a mode of utilization appropriate for their context.
- Designed an LNRA for an upcoming educational event in their context.

How? (Learning tasks and materials)

Learning Task 1: A Sample LNRA

1A. In pairs, review this LNRA, which was used for this workshop.

Thank you for responding to this short needs assessment survey for the workshop on Learning Needs and Resources Assessment that will be held at this year's MEDED Conference in Philadelphia. Please send your answer to Dr. Vella by reply e-mail before June 1st.

    a. How do you usually do a needs assessment with students or trainees?

    b. What one thing would you hope to learn in a workshop on cutting edge methods of needs assessment?

Tell your partner what your response was when you
received this survey.

Name one way you would change this learning needs and
resources survey. We'll hear a sample.

Learning Task 2: What Is an LNRA?

In new pairs, read this description and circle what strikes you as
useful in your context.

> The learning needs and resources assessment begins the dialogue
> before the course or training. It is a way to discover the resources
> in the group as well as their perceived learning needs. It *informs* a
> course design; it does not *form* it. That is, learners do not decide
> what they are to learn. They have a consultative voice, offering
> suggestions on the final design. The teacher, professor, facilitator,
> or course designer has the deliberative or decisive voice, making
> the final decisions on what is to be taught. These decisions are
> informed by data from the LNRA.

Share what you have circled in the table group. We'll hear a
sample.

Learning Task 3: Rules of Design

3A. In new pairs, read over these guidelines for designing an
LNRA:

Short is sweet.

Aim it at resources as well as needs.

Invite as much background information as possible; for
example, *Where do you work? What is your responsibility?
What do you need to do your job?*

3B. In the same pairs, decide what you would add to this list as
a guideline for designing an LNRA in your context. We'll
hear a sample.

Learning Task 4: LNRA Modes of Utilization

Read over this list of LNRA modes of utilization. Decide on one (or add to the list one of your own devising) and design questions for an LNRA for an upcoming course you are teaching. Share your LNRA and mode of utilization at your table.

Modes of utilization:

LNRA

E-mail survey

Web registration survey

Registration survey sent by mail—longer

Telephone call interview

Interview following observation on the job

Learning Task 5: Value Added?

In pairs, describe what you see as value added when you do a learning needs and resources assessment of students or patients or professional colleagues prior to an educational event. We'll hear a sample.

Advanced Learning Design Course, Raleigh, North Carolina

The Advanced Learning Design Course is a course for those who have been using dialogue education for some years One of the sessions reviews the potential of the learning task.

Four Parts of the Learning Task

Who? (The participants)

Eight dialogue educators.

Why? (The situation)

These men and women have taken the initial course *Learning to Listen, Learning to Teach* some years before. They have been designing using dialogue education, and need to confirm and enhance their own skills. They bring their selected dialogue education designs to this course, and have read *Taking Learning to Task* (Vella, 2001) in preparation.

When? (The time frame)

Two hours on day one of the course.

Where? (The site)

A room with tables for small-group work.

What? (The content)

- Chapter Four in *Taking Learning to Task.*
- The four elements of a learning task.
- The flow and sequence of these four elements.
- Modes of "input".

What for? (Achievement-based objectives)

By the end of this two-hour session, all will have

- Named the four elements of a learning task from their contexts.
- Examined the flow and sequence of these parts.
- Identified diverse modes of "input".
- Redesigned a learning task in their portfolio.

How? (Learning tasks and materials)

Learning Task 1: Taking Learning to Task

1A. Read over Chapter Four of *Taking Learning to Task*. In pairs, tell what is new for you in this chapter and what you see is an important reminder. We'll hear all.

1B. Name one principle from this chapter that you have used. We'll hear all.

Learning Task 2: Four Elements of a Learning Task

In pairs, review these four elements of a learning task:

Inductive work

Input

Implementation

Integration

These have also been named *anchor*, *add*, *apply*, and *away*. Name these parts in your own words, considering how you have used them in your work so far. We'll hear all.

Learning Task 3: Flow and Sequence of These Elements

3A. In new pairs, consider what a rearrangement of these elements will do. For example, consider what happens to learning when you put *input* first. Share your rearrangements and consequences at your table.

3B. *A learning task is an open question put to a small group, with all the resources needed to respond.* In new pairs, name ways in which this applies to each of these elements in order. We'll hear all.

Learning Task 4: Redesigning Our Own Work

4A. Select a learning task from your own design. Redesign it to use what you have just learned about the potential of the four elements Share your redesign at your table.

4B. Name one advantage of considering these four elements as your design. We'll hear all.

Implementation Challenge 11A: Face-to-Face

These four examples are all of face-to-face courses. Consider a face-to-face course you are about to design. Name one advantage you see in the use of the seven design steps and the four elements of learning tasks.

Implementation Challenge 11B: On-Line

Identify one thing you found in this chapter that can be used in the design of an on-line course. The next chapter presents an example of an on-line course using dialogue education.

12

AN ON-LINE COURSE USING DIALOGUE EDUCATION

Is virtual dialogue possible?

The example in this chapter offers a design for one section in a course on adult education principles and practices in a graduate course of fourteen weeks. I thank Sarah Swart of University of Detroit Mercy for her modeling and managing of an on-line course in summer 2006. Our rich experience together proved that dialogue is never *virtual*, but always real and nourishing. The chapter closes with "My Turn"—my comments on the process.

Seven Design Steps

Who? (The participants)

Adult educators and candidates for a master's degree in adult education.

Why? (The situation)

These men and women have heard of dialogue education and have read some of Jane Vella's work. They need to experience dialogue education enough to use the seven design steps in planning a course and to design and lead learning tasks.

When? (The time frame)

Asynchronous on-line learning for one week, the tenth in a fourteen-week overview adult education graduate course; two hours synchronous work: one hour each Monday and Friday.

Where? (The site)

The Internet—a virtual world.

What? (The content)

- The roots of dialogue education: Freire, Lewin, Mezirow.
- Seven design steps.
- The four elements of a learning task: inductive, input, implementation, integration.
- Texts: *Learning to Listen, Learning to Teach; Taking Learning to Task.*

What for? (Achievement-based objectives)

By the end of this tenth week in the course, the participants will have

- Examined the roots of dialogue education: Freire, Lewin.
- Reviewed the seven design steps.
- Defined and described learning tasks, including the four elements: inductive, input, implementation, integration.

How? (Learning tasks and materials)

These are part of the on-line course.

Learning Task 1: The Roots of Dialogue Education
1A. In the discussion group, describe ways in which dialogue has enhanced your learning or your teaching so far.

1B. Go to www.globalearning.com and read *What Is Dialogue Education?* Go to http://www.infed.org/thinkers/et-freir .htm, read the entire article, and go to one link. Go to http://www.infed.org/thinkers/et-lewin.htm and read the entire article.

1C. Write a single paragraph showing how Freire and Lewin seem to you to be coming from the same roots. Share that on the discussion group page.

1D. Read the preface, pages ix–xxi, of *Learning to Listen, Learning to Teach.* Name one way that this dialogue education approach might work in your context. Share this perception in the discussion group.

Learning Task 2: The Seven Design Steps

2A. Consider the way you plan a class or a course now. Sketch the elements of that system for yourself for comparison with the seven design steps.

2B. Read pages 37–47 of *Learning to Listen, Learning to Teach* (Vella, 2002). Circle those elements in this reading that seem most useful to you. Share what you circled in the discussion group.

2C. Select a course you are about to offer. Name the *Who?* (participants and leaders), *Why?* (the situation that calls for the course), *When?* (the time frame), *Where?* (the site), *What?* (one or two items of content—nouns), *What for?* (achievement-based objectives—"they will have . . . "), and *How?* (one learning task and necessary materials). Put your design on the discussion page for review.

2D. Write one paragraph that details what you see as the advantage of using the seven design steps. Put that on the discussion page. Talk to Jane Vella in the chat room about your use of this planning tool.

Learning Task 3: Learning Tasks and the Four Elements

3A. Consider all the learning tasks you have just completed in this week: 1A, B, C, D, 2A, B, C, D. How did these discrete tasks help you to learn? Write one paragraph for the discussion page.

3B. Read all of *Taking Learning to Task* (Vella, 2001) or at least pages 33–48 on the use of learning tasks. Ask your questions of Jane Vella during the chat room time or post them on the discussion page for her review and response.

3C. Consider the learning task you prepared for 2C. Identify the *inductive* element, the *input*, the *implementation work*, and the *integration* element in your learning task. Write a paragraph for the discussion page on this for review and response.

3D. What are your hopes for using learning tasks in your future teaching? Write one paragraph on this for the discussion page.

Although this example demonstrates only one section and only one week of work in a larger on-line graduate course, I see advantages in the precise learning tasks; their visible, demonstrable, and reviewable products; and in the integration of all three parts of the content.

An on-line course cannot take the place of the experiential, communal introductory course *Learning to Listen, Learning to Teach*, just as we would not want our surgeon to have learned his skills on-line. Any book has a classic place in learning, sacred and unchallenged. An on-line course has its place in learning, still undetermined and surely challenged. An experiential course has its place in learning as well, a place as sacred as any book.

It is our great advantage in this critical century in human history to make all of these—books, experiential face-to-face courses, on-line courses—work together for effective learning.

13

DIALOGUE EDUCATION IN SCHOOL LEADERSHIP

We teach the way we have been taught.

This chapter presents an example from Utah's Institute for Sustainable Leadership (UISL) and the Utah Staff Development Council (USDC), where dialogue education is used to design and lead a workshop for educators, administrators, principals, and school staff. When Christelle Estrada was president of the Utah Staff Development Council, she read *Learning to Listen, Learning to Teach* and found the website www.globalearning .com, which showed where she could study how to implement the dialogue education approach. After completing the initial course in Raleigh, North Carolina, Estrada took what she had learned back to her colleagues at USDC. You will read here *selections* from the course she designed. The full professional development course is now being offered to educators throughout Utah.

Christine Huley of USDC described the initial response of USDC staff: "We were stunned when we were asked not to make our customary presentations with our excellent PowerPoint slides, but instead to design a course that would engage learners and teach them accountably so that they could use what they learned back in their schools."

Institute for Sustainable Leadership

Note how thoroughly contextualized this design is. The USDC staff have taken the essentials of dialogue education and made it fit their unique set of participants and the unique situation of Utah.

Notice, too, in this design how thoroughly all that is to be taught is explicitly described. Notice how they have correlated the content, the achievement-based objectives, and the learning tasks and materials. Such correlation, in careful sequence, is a source of accountability. Learners leave the two-day session knowing that they know because they have just done something significant with their new learning.

The Seven Design Steps

Who? (participants, leaders)

Thirty principals, administrators, teachers, and aides from different school districts; two staff from Professional Learning.

Why? (the situation)

The goal of the Utah Staff Development Council is to create a collaborative network that challenges all adults to support students in being successful in every aspect of their lives. Because USDC is focusing efforts on a two-year initiative that emphasizes sustainable leadership for the twenty-first century through equity and excellence, they asked, How can we best respond to the needs of adult learners and provide high-quality professional learning to build capacity for distributive and sustainable leadership to benefit all students in Utah? These thirty participants need to experience a way of management and teaching for equity and excellence based on dialogue education.

When? (time frame)

Two days; sixteen hours.

Where: (site)

Utah Professional Training Center—a large room with tables for small-group work, two easels, a projector, large screen, and laptop.

What? (content)

1. Value of warm-ups
2. How adults learn
3. Twelve principles for adult learning
4. Learning tasks
5. Principles of feedback
6. How to give and receive feedback
7. Team collaboration
8. Learning needs and resources assessment
9. Seven steps of design
10. Learning and transfer

What for? (Achievement-based objectives)

By the end of this two-day session, all will have

- Participated in warm-ups and named their value for learning.
- Examined adult learning principles and applied them to their own contexts (situations).
- Identified the distinctions among the four learning tasks and designed a learning task most relevant to their contexts.
- Identified the qualities for giving and receiving feedback from personal experience, compared and contrasted to research, and identified opportunities for feedback in their own contexts.
- Assessed their collaboration and facilitation skills and planned for continuous growth with systematic feedback.
- Determined what they can do to assess the learning needs and resources in their contexts and designed an LNRA for an adult student learning experience.
- Reviewed Vella's seven design steps.
- Used the seven steps to design the adult student learning experience for their own contexts, showing learning and transfer.

How? (Learning tasks)

Day One

- Task 1 – Warm-up: Our Stories
- Task 2 – Program Review: Achievement-Based Objectives
- Task 3 – Group Culture: Developing Norms
- Task 4 – How Adults Learn
- Task 5 – Four Elements in a Learning Task
- Task 6 – Principles of Feedback: Giving and Receiving
- Task 7 – Team Collaboration: Putting It All Together

Day Two

- Task 8 – Learning Needs and Resources Assessments (LNRA)
- Task 9 – Seven Steps of Design
- Task 10 – Learning and Transfer: Planning for the Adult Learning Experience with Site Teams
- Task 11 – Creating a Feedback-Rich Environment
- Task 12 – Implementation and Integration: Designing Ongoing Teamwork
- Task 13 – Benefits and Commitment

Day One: Welcome and Introductions

Learning Task 1: Warm-up: Our Stories

1A. Name a student who has influenced your learning. Describe the situation. Then name what you see as the common characteristics in your stories.

1B. Write your student's name on the strip of cloth in front of you. When you introduce yourself (name and school/district), also say the name of your student.

Learning Task 2: Program Review: ABOs

2A. Read the ABOs (*What for?*) in the seven design steps for this two-day institute. With a partner, name one or two of these that are most immediately relevant to you. Share with a new partner why you think those learnings would benefit you in your current situation.

2B. Write each one you named on a sticky note. Read aloud from each note. Then place it on our Achievement-Based Objectives Select Chart.

Learning Task 3: Group Culture: Developing Norms

Read these norms developed for the Utah Staff Development Council. With the same partner, identify one *other* behavior that you believe would benefit the learning of the group. Write each on a sticky note and read aloud it as you post your note on our norms chart.

USDC Norms

Watch your own airtime: how often and how long you speak.

Assumption: It is important to hear all voices. Each member of the group will monitor his own behavior. Each person's perspective makes a contribution to the group. The facilitator will create space and time for those who have not spoken to speak if they choose.

Assumption: The role of the facilitator is to *create* the conditions for maximum input and reflection and to *model* facilitation strategies that could be used in other contexts. Suspend your personal agenda and focus on supporting the achievement of the stated objectives of the meeting.

Assumption: We are all learners. We can create new learning together.

Learning Task 4: How Adults Learn

ABO: You will have examined adult learning principles and applied them to your own context (situation).

4A. Review the list of adult learning principles that follow. Circle the three most important principles that you personally need as an adult learner.

4B. In threes, share what you circled and what you discovered about your own adult learning needs and these principles. We'll hear a sample.

Principles of Adult Learning

1. *Needs Assessment:* participation of the learners in naming what is to be learned. Listening to learners' wants and needs helps shape a program that has immediate usefulness to adults.

2. *Safety* in the environment and the process. We create a context for learning by ensuring that the environment is nonjudgmental. Allowing small groups to find their voices.

3. *Sound relationships among learners:* we can nurture each other's thinking power by affirmation of the person. Other people are in relationships with us—it is up to us to determine what kind of relationship it is.

4. *Sequence of content and reinforcement:* using a design that goes from simple to complex and builds in time for reinforcing new learning.

5. *Praxis:* action with reflection or learning by doing. Each learner re-creates the content through participation.

6. *Respect for learners as decision makers:* ensuring that learners are subjects of their own learning by making their own decisions. Don't ever do what the learner can do.

7. *Ideas, feelings, and actions:* cognitive, affective, and psycho-motor aspects of learning.

8. *Immediacy of the learning:* to see the immediate usefulness of new learning. Learners deciding on the significance and application of the new skill.

9. *Clear roles and role development:* reinforcement of the human equity among learners. Moving adults to learn together in dialogue.

10. *Teamwork:* the process and design must include all learners. We live in a participatory universe. Learning is enhanced by peers.

11. *Engagement of the learners in what they are learning:* open questions invite "both-and" thinking and dialogue. Product is dependent on process. Learning demands energy.

12. *Accountability:* learners are accountable to their colleagues and themselves and to agreed-upon ways of working together. The design of learning events must be accountable to the learners.

Source: Adapted from Vella, 2002.

Small-Group Work. Notice how all of the learning tasks in this program are implemented in small groups. The small group is the locus of learning; however, the learning is always individual. Each participant is totally engaged and relating all new input to his or her context. Notice how USDC has integrated new content into the patterns of dialogue education, using the principles and practices to teach all of the content. Notice how input is offered in a variety of modes. Content is always ascribed to the source.

Learning Task 5: Four Elements in a Learning Task

ABO: You will have identified the distinctions between the four elements in a learning task, and you will have designed a learning task for your context.

5A. In pairs, look back at the learning tasks we have done this morning. Tell one way these were useful to you. We'll hear a sample.

5B. Review the following description of learning tasks and the four elements:

A learning task is an open question put to a small group, with all the resources they need to respond. Learning tasks have a natural sequence of four elements:

Inductive work: Connecting the new content to the learners' lives

Input: The new content

Implementation: Doing something with the new content in order to comprehend it

Integration: Taking the new content into one's own context; testing it there

5C. Looking back at the learning tasks done today, in pairs, name those that seem to be inductive, those that involve input, those that are implementation tasks and, those that move to integration. We'll hear a sample of what you name.

5D. In new pairs, sketch a brief learning task using the four parts identified in 5B to teach each other the history of your school district. Remember that verbs in a learning task are active and specific: identify, circle, review, list, name, select. Post your four-element learning task on the board for all to see and celebrate.

Learning Task 6: Principles of Feedback: Giving and Receiving

ABO: You will have identified the qualities for giving and receiving feedback from personal experience, compared and contrasted to research, and identified opportunities for feedback in your own context.

6A. *Characteristics of feedback.* Share with one other person at your table a story about receiving feedback. Identify common feelings about the experience. We'll hear a sample.

6B. *Research on feedback.* Read the following research on giving and receiving feedback. Circle the sections that you find most useful. We'll hear a sample of what you circled.

Giving Feedback

Useful feedback is

1. *Invited by the recipient.* Feedback is most effective when requested. This provides the opportunity for the recipient to set the parameters for the feedback.

2. *Given with care.* To be useful, feedback requires the giver to be a genuine advocate for the learning of the person receiving feedback.

3. *Given with attention.* The giver needs to be aware of *both* the recipient's responses, verbal and nonverbal, and the giver's own responses as well as tone of voice and choice of words.

4. *Directly expressed.* The most useful feedback is open, direct, and concrete. Valuable feedback is specific and clear, dealing with particular incidents and behaviors.

5. *Uncluttered by evaluative judgments.* Feedback that is descriptive is the most effective.

6. *Readily actionable.* Feedback focusing on changed behavior instead of matters outside the control of the recipient is valuable.

7. *Well-timed and in an appropriate place.* Feedback should be given with sufficient time and space to be considered by the recipient, away from others. It should be close to the particular event being discussed.

8. *Confidential.* All information discussed should not be shared unless permission is asked and given.

9. *Checked and clarified.* Checking perceptions and seeking clarity of context with the recipient before feedback is essential.

10. Made by *speaking for oneself.* When giving feedback, share only those things that are directly observed.

Source: Adapted from Streibel, Joiner, and Scholtes, 2003.

Receiving Feedback

1. *Breathe.* Taking full breaths will help your body relax and your brain focus.

2. *Be specific.* Use a framing question to identify the concrete behavior about which you want feedback.

3. *Listen carefully.* Suspend your judgments about what the person is saying. Do not interrupt or justify.

4. *Clarify your understanding of the feedback.* Is it a fit? Does it make sense? Ask for specific examples.

5. *Summarize your understanding of the feedback.* Paraphrase what you have heard so that the person giving feedback will know that you have understood what was communicated.

6. *Take time to sort out what you hear.* Processing feedback is important if you are to take action on it. A major element in receiving feedback is observing the emotions that feedback brings up.

Source: Adapted from Bushardt and Fowler, 2003.

6C. *Creating a feedback-rich environment.* Individually, make a list of two or three opportunities you could create to ask for feedback. Identify someone who can provide the kind of feedback you want. Share one or more items from your list with a partner.

Learning Task 7: Team Collaboration: Putting It All Together
ABO: You will have used the first day's learning experiences to generate ideas for increased adult collaboration to support *all* students in being successful. You will have offered feedback on day one.

7A. *Debrief the day.* Each member of the table group team shares a key learning from today. Tell how you hope to use what was learned. We'll hear a sample.

7B. *Feedback—day one.* Write your responses to these four open questions. This information will help us shape day two. Share what you have written at your table, and give the course leaders your papers.

What worked for you as a learner?

What didn't work for you as a learner?

What questions do you still have from today's learning?

What additional comments, insights, or ideas can you share with us?

Congruence. Notice how congruent the designers and leaders are with the principles they are teaching. They invite feedback with open questions, and show that they intend to use what they hear to amend the program.

Notice the verbs used throughout the learning tasks: they are all tough, specific action verbs. See Appendix B for more such verbs.

Day Two

Learning Task 8: Learning Needs and Resources Assessments
ABO: You will have determined what you can do to assess the learning needs and resources in your context and designed an LNRA for an adult student learning experience.

8A. In pairs, describe the usefulness to you of the learning needs and resources assessment that you completed in preparation for this institute. We'll hear a sample.

8B. Review this description of the learning needs and resources assessment (LNRA) from the work of Jane Vella (adapted from *Learning to Listen, Learning to Teach,* 2002, and *Taking Learning to Task,* 2001).

LNRA is a process through which the teacher learns and then makes explicit for learners their themes, issues, and questions around the topic being taught. Tom Hutchinson's (1978) WWW question is always useful: *Who* needs *what* as defined by *whom*? During a needs assessment, the designer of a program can see and hear what kinds of learning tasks a group needs and wants. If the program addresses real needs, the learning task has immediacy. Attention to the culture of a set of learners is a form of respect. Such attention can elicit the data needed to design appropriate learning tasks. All that we ask is attention to the cultural mores of your learners. This attention can be demonstrated, and the data gathered, through a simple learning needs and resources assessment.

8C. *LNRA for you.* Circle one element about the LNRA in the preceding paragraph that is significant for you. Share your reason with a partner. We will hear a sample.

8D. In pairs, write at least three questions for an LNRA for an upcoming class or staff development workshop you are planning. Post your draft LNRA. We will hear a sample of your LNRA.

Learning Task 9: Seven Steps of Design

ABO: You will have reviewed Vella's seven design steps and used them to plan a session.

9A. Review the seven design steps previously used for this program and the following description of the seven steps.

Who? Who is coming to this program? What do they do? What experiences have they had related to this topic? Ages? Position? Include anything that could have a bearing on the design decisions you make.

Why? Name the situation that calls for this training. Think of it in terms of the learners' needs, not what you (the leader) need to do.

When? Time frame (such as thirty minutes), time of day, what part of the day or week.

Where? Location, characteristics of the space—anything that might make a difference to your design.

What? The content of the program—the knowledge, skills, or attitudes (SKAs). What they need to learn.

What for? (Achievement-based objectives) What they will do with the content to learn it during the learning session

How? (Learning tasks) How the ABOs will be accomplished by the learners.

9B. In pairs, sketch just the first six design steps for an upcoming professional development session: *Who? Why ? When? Where? What? What for?*

Share your designs at the table. Then post your draft design. We'll hear a sample.

Learning Task 10: Learning and Transfer: Planning for the Adult Learning Experience with Site Teams

ABO: You will have completed the *How?* of the seven design steps to begin the design for an adult learning experience for your own context.

In your pairs, design at least one learning task to teach one of the content pieces in your design. Share your designs at the table. Then post your draft design. We'll hear all.

Learning Task 11: Creating a Feedback-Rich Environment

ABO: You will have practiced giving and receiving feedback on initial plans by implementing the principles of effective feedback.

Two pairs work together to give feedback on each other's seven design steps, using the following comment and suggestion formats:

I really liked . . . because . . .

How about . . . ? (offer suggestions for changes)

The team receiving feedback responds to both comments and suggestions with "Thank you!"

Deliberative and Consultative Voices. Notice that those giving feedback do so in a consultative voice: offering suggestions. Ultimately, those who receive feedback have the deliberative or decisive voice as they decide what part of the feedback to use.

Learning Task 12: Implementation and Integration: Designing Ongoing Teamwork

ABO: You will have assessed personal learning and team learning to design future work while identifying the necessary support from USDC.

Strengths and Challenges

12A. Using the ABOs of the Institute, identify the areas that are now strengths and those that are still challenges.

12B. At your table, generate ideas about how USDC could support your growth as a team or as an individual. We'll hear and document all.

12C. Identify one idea about possible future work together. We'll hear and document all.

Learning Task 13: Benefits and Commitment

ABO: You will have identified a new learning for yourself and made a commitment to apply it in your specific context.

Giving the Gift of Your Learning

Identify the most significant learning for you during these two days. Now identify a child or adult who will benefit from your learning.

Using the postcard in front of you, write that person's name and explain to yourself how you will use your learning for her or him.

Address the postcard to yourself.

When all are finished, take turns standing and reading the name of the child or adult who will receive the gift of this new learning.

Put your card in the large envelope labeled POSTCARDS. We will mail your postcard you sometime in the future!

Reflections on the Use of Dialogue Education

Consider the difference between the sample of this conference that you have just read and the usual two-day staff development conference, where facilitators offer "presentations" on relevant issues with supportive PowerPoint slides. Estrada's use of dialogue education in this conference means that learners were fully engaged, worked in small groups, and developed relevant and useful materials for their own programs. How do they know they know? They did it.

What follows are reflections of two Utah Staff Development Council members who were invited by Estrada to use this dialogue education approach in their work. It was, as they note, an uncomfortable shift.

Reflection: Sydnee S. Dickson

The first level of learning, transfer, and impact for me has been self-awareness and dramatic personal change. When I was asked to cofacilitate this material, I felt ill-equipped. I had read several books by Jane Vella and was intrigued by the work; however, I found myself feeling uncomfortable sitting in a room without posters, with only a visual of our intended outcomes. I was told by my friend and mentor, Christelle Estrada, the room would be filled with learners' work before long. Armed with nothing but a binder of materials, a pencil and a highlighter, we set out. I had determined to gauge the success of our experience based on the feedback from the most cynical participants in the room. I was certain this experience wouldn't work for many of the participants.

Halfway through the day I started feeling agitated. I could understand where my discomfort was coming from. I left the session discouraged, irritated, and confused. Sometime that evening I felt a shock wave permeate my being. It became very clear to me that my discomfort was in realizing that there is a more powerful way to engage adult learners and that I had just experienced that type of learning. What I had previously labeled as active learning was indeed passive learning. A death and rebirth occurred over the next twenty-four hours. It was what Freire called "the death of the professor."

The shelves in my office are still heavily laden with very organized binders full of overheads that will most likely never see the light of day. PowerPoints are stored on disks and memory sticks. In their place is a simple template called "The Seven Steps of Design." By [our] assessing the needs of the participants and the students they serve, then designing learning tasks based on these needs, powerful learning is occurring on a daily basis for adults in our system. So how does this look different than traditional professional development? Small teams of teachers are bringing their personal work to the table (including student data and lesson plans) and engaging in reflective conversation about how they can meet the diverse learning needs of their students. Lesson design begins with achievement based outcomes. New ideas come from problem solving and research and are formulated into lesson plans that are immediately utilized in the classroom.

New strategies are finding their way into traditional education settings. Doors of collaboration are open wider than ever before. School leaders are finding that they can "cover" more in faculty meetings by engaging staff members in the work through learning tasks. This is due in part to the fact that they have voluntarily come together this year to study the topic of "change" through the use of learning tasks. Book study (such as *Results Now* by Mike

Schmoker) is conducted through text rendering, conversation, and reflection, and learning tasks take the topics to a personal and useful level. Teachers and school leaders are becoming intolerant of being "talked at." PowerPoints have become power "pointless." Teacher leadership teams in schools are using learning tasks in faculty meetings and other professional development settings to engage their peers in new learning, problem solving and school planning.

Perhaps one of the most powerful experiences has been working for a brief period of time with superintendents from around the state. I was asked to "present" the National Staff Development Council (NSDC) Standards to them and discuss their role as leaders of professional development efforts in their districts. I "warned" them ahead of time that this wouldn't be a presentation and that the expectation would be for them to be active participants who would guide their own learning. A needs assessment helped me determine that they had little knowledge of the NSDC Standards but were interested in learning more. Through a text-rendering warm-up, an input task that included viewing a rubric of the standards and an implementation task based on interaction with a peer, powerful learning occurred. All Superintendents who were present are now familiar with the NSDC Standards and can articulate their role in leading professional development efforts. This was all done through personal reading, reflection, and conversation. Members of this group are now asking us to replicate a similar experience with their district leaders. Leaders of this group have asked for more conversation and less presentation in their meetings.

The professor is dead and buried in the Professional Learning Department in Granite School District, Utah. New teachers, their mentors, coaches, principals, school leadership teams, and classroom teachers are transferring practice at higher rates than ever before due to the use of adult learning principles. As we strive for a change of heart within and among ourselves and others, we hope to recapture meaning and purpose for all educators.

Reflection: Christine Huley

When I first came on board in the professional learning office I was used to "looking chic in my Ann Taylor outfit" and leading the "charge" for professional development with principals and teachers. Syd Dickson and I would plan the professional development, using PowerPoint and trying our best to facilitate "activities" that would engage the participants. Our method for evaluating the impact was always an evaluation form which attempted to assess how they would use the content back at their schools and what "next steps" they might want. We never really knew for certain whether our facilitation and presentation made a difference for the adult learner. We tried our best and our intentions were in the right place. The professional development was about "me," and my personality actually liked the attention and "being on stage" and knowing more than the audience . . . so I thought!

Then Christelle Estrada entered our lives and changes were about to happen! The Utah Staff Development Council is an affiliate of the National Staff Development Council, and at the time, Christelle was the affiliate president for USDC. Our meetings changed drastically. Instead of "running the meeting" Christelle began with a warm-up and connected us to the work at hand. She slowly introduced us to the work of Jane Vella by having us "do the work." For example, we were introduced to the principles of adult learning by, first, starting with an inductive task, then identifying the principles most important to us and debriefing on the implications this would have in our work with adults. To be honest, for me, the switch to doing with learning tasks and clear outcomes was uncomfortable at first. I realized that I wanted "someone" to run the meeting which would allow me to be a "passive" participant. It was scary to have to take risks in my own learning, but safety in the environment was always present.

It did not take long for USDC to decide that we wanted to offer teams of adults this knowledge (principles of adult learning, seven steps of design, and learning tasks) through the lens of Fullan's Eight Principles of Sustainable Leadership. Christelle Estrada designed the institute and Syd and I were asked to cofacilitate a group of twenty-five adults with another colleague who was skilled in dialogue education.

I was thinking about the adult learners and how they were going to respond to a professional learning experience that was very different from what they were used to—the "sage on the stage" approach. Again, I felt discomfort as we began the two-day institute. As time went on, the power of the intentionality of the work, the fact that we conducted a needs assessment up front, a warm-up that connected the adult learner to a student who made a difference in their life—and then moving forward to learning tasks that engaged and held the learner accountable to their learning. From an observational standpoint, the adults were "doing what they were learning." Relevance and immediacy was provided by the teams selecting a principle (Fullan) that they could build upon back at their context. Accountability and feedback was provided, and the closure involved "thinking about a person who will benefit from the learning of the institute," and a postcard was provided for each participant to send to themselves a thought about the work they had undertaken (which would be sent to them in the future). The institute was designed around and honored the adult. It was a beautiful experience and changed the way that I view myself as a facilitator of adult learning.

We do *teach the way we were taught.* You see in this selection from the School Leadership Course that these school administrators are being taught in a new way. They are making a difference in the schools of Utah.

14

DIALOGUE EDUCATION IN HEALTH CARE SETTINGS

Patients are learners, too.

Much adult education takes place in health care settings. Patient education is a significant and growing discipline. As a septuagenarian, I have been an impatient patient at the hands of doctors, nurses, and health educators who were using an educational approach that did not involve the principles of dialogue education.

This chapter offers three examples of dialogue education in health care settings. The first is a simple one-hour program designed for senior citizens at a YMCA, introducing them to a valuable text by teaching one set of cogent facts about nutrition. The second is a simple course in nutrition for young mothers-to-be. The third is a program for seniors featuring Resources for Seniors.

A Short Program on Food and Stress

This dialogue education program can be used in senior citizen programs everywhere. Notice the sound content offered and learned, and the engagement of all learners.

The Seven Design Steps

Who? (The participants)

YMCA nutrition class: twenty men and women, all seniors.

Why? (The situation)

These senior citizens need to discover ways to deal with stress, to help control their weight and prevent strokes and other diseases of aging. This initial one-hour session will introduce them to the text *You: On a Diet* by Michael Roizen and Mehmet Oz (2006) by teaching content from Chapter Four. A twelve-session course will follow, teaching the whole book.

When? (The time frame)

A one-hour class: sixty minutes.

Where? (The site)

A classroom at the YMCA with tables for small-group work, a whiteboard, and a flip chart on an easel.

What? (The contents)

- Introduction to the text *You: On a Diet*.
- The difference between nuclear factor kappa B (NFKappa B) and paroxisome proliferator-activated receptors (PPARs).
- Food sources of paroxisome proliferator-activated receptors PPARs.

What for? (Achievement-based objectives)

By the end of this hour, all will have:

- Named their experience with diets and their hope for learning from this book.
- Read and responded to an excerpt from the text on inflammation, anti-inflammatory and antioxidant food sources.
- Named ways they can use this information today. Indicated what else they need to know.
- Proposed a shopping list for tomorrow.

You: On a Diet assumes that readers have all been on a diet and somehow have been disappointed. The authors invite us to learn the biological processes of digestion and to make decisions about food that will support healthy processes.

How? (Learning tasks)

Learning Task 1 (inductive work): What a Waist!
1A.   In pairs, share your experience with dieting.

1B.   Name one thing you'd like to learn about food and eating habits that could free you from dieting. We'll hear all.

Learning Task 2 (input)
Read the following extract from *You: On a Diet*. Circle what you find most useful. We'll hear what you circled.

> Your liver takes every chemical in your body and processes it by binding it to a protein, transforming it into something your body can use. In your liver, nutrients can be met by two substances. One is from foods that release *nuclear factor kappa B* (NF kappa B) which triggers a chain of events that causes inflammation in the digestive system. The other substance, *paroxisome proliferator-activated receptors* PPAR's), are from foods that have an anti-inflammatory effect.
>
> Your best weapon against fat is good food—inflammation-reducing food. To reduce obesity-causing inflammation, you need to eat foods with nutrients that can do just that, by having direct anti-inflammatory or antioxidant properties or by stimulating the PPARs and inhibiting the NF kappa Bs [Roizen and Oz, p. 89].
>
> • Substances known to fight inflammation:
>
> • Omega 3 fatty acids found in fish oils (three four-ounce servings of fish per week)
>
> • Green tea (three glasses a day)
>
> • Beer—one drink per day
>
> • Turmeric—A pinch of turmeric (1/8 of a teaspoon) per day

- Coffee
- Bananas [Roizen and Oz, 2006, pp. 95–96]

Learning Task 3 (implementation)

3A. In pairs, decide what you can do with this information from the text *You: On a Diet*. We'll hear a sample.

3B. What more would you like to hear from these doctors and this book? We'll hear a sample.

Learning Task 4 (integration)

4A. In pairs, list the items from this short introductory session that you want to do further research on, either in the library or on your computer. We'll hear all.

4B. In family groups, prepare a shopping list that will use what has been learned here today. Include a trip to the library or bookstore for *You: On a Diet*. We'll hear a sample.

Notice how crisp and succinct the learning tasks are. This is an introduction not only to the text but also to this process of adult learning via dialogue. Their experience has to be one of significant and immediate learning, so that real, healthy transfer takes place. Only this will motivate senior citizens to attend a longer course.

Notice how the content from the text has been formatted for accessibility and ready comprehension. Notice how every learning task is an open question, put to the small groups with all the resources they need to respond. How do they know they know this specific content? They just did something meaningful with it, together, in a safe environment.

A One-Day Workshop for Expectant Mothers

Research discoveries relate to real people in real need. The power of folic acid to prevent birth defects is very important learning for a pregnant woman and her husband and family. However, this learning can be offered as inaccessible jargon, diminishing the woman's sense of herself and her potential for learning and preventative action. Dialogue education, in its design and teaching mode, make this learning accessible and useful to learners at every level, without in any way reducing the research findings.

The Seven Design Steps

Who? (The participants)

Five hundred young women in a university biology class.

Why? (The situation)

These women are at an age when they might get pregnant. They need to know the value of folic acid and how to access it through their diet. This class is part of a Women's Nutrition Section of Biology. This two-hour class will introduce them to the uses and sources of folic acid and help them see how vital it is in prevention of birth defects.

When? (The time frame)

A two -hour college class.

Where? (The site)

A large hall in the science building of a university. A projection computer and a large screen.

What? (The contents)

- Signs of folic acid deficiency.
- Centers for Disease Control mandates about folic acid and pregnancy.

- Sources of folic acid.
- Suggestions for sharing this learning.

What for? (Achievement-based objectives)

By the end of these two hours, all will have

- Identified signs of folic acid deficiency.
- Reviewed a list of source foods.
- Prepared a diet for a pregnant woman.
- Named three reasons every young woman should be getting folic acid.
- Suggested ways of getting this word out.

How? (Learning tasks)

Learning Task 1: How Are You Feeling?
Read this short note on folic acid deficiency.

Signs Of Folic Acid Deficiency
The signs of folic acid deficiency can be subtle. You may have diarrhea, loss of appetite, and weight loss, as well as weakness, a sore tongue, headaches, heart palpitations, and irritability. If you're only mildly deficient, you may not notice any symptoms at all, but you won't be getting the optimal amount you need for your baby's early embryonic development. That's why all women of child-bearing age need to take folic acid, even if they feel perfectly well [BabyCenter, n.d.].

In pairs, decide what you would say to a friend who complained of any of these signs. We'll hear all.

Learning Task 2 (input)
2A. Read the following discussion of food sources of folic acid:

What Are the Best Food Sources?

Food manufacturers are required by the Food and Drug Administration to add folic acid to enriched grain products such as breakfast cereals, bread, pasta, and rice so that each serving contains at least 20 percent of the daily requirement, and some breakfast cereals contain 100 percent (400 mcg) or more. Some examples: Grape-Nuts (50 percent), Wheatena (10 percent). Dark leafy greens are also a good source of folate, as are legumes such as lentils and chick-peas. Other sources include the following:

> 1/2 cup cooked lentils: 179 mcg
>
> 1 cup boiled collard greens: 177 mcg
>
> 1/2 cup canned chickpeas: 141 mcg
>
> 1 papaya: 115 mcg
>
> 1 orange: 39 mcg
>
> 1 cup cooked frozen peas: 94 mcg
>
> 4 spears steamed or boiled asparagus: 88 mcg
>
> 1/2 cup steamed broccoli: 52 mcg
>
> 1 cup strawberries: 40 mcg [BabyCenter, n.d.]

2B.   You need 400 mcg of folic acid per day prior to pregnancy. In pairs, make up a daily diet for yourselves from this list that ensures that intake. We'll hear a sample.

Learning Task 3: Facts About Folates

3A.   Read these notes from the CDC. Circle or note what is important to you. We'll hear a sample of what you circled or noted.

Once you're pregnant, you'll need at least 600 mcg daily, although many practitioners suggest 800 mcg and some prenatal vitamins contain 1,000 mcg. Folic acid is a water-soluble vitamin, so your body will flush out the excess if you take too much. . . .

If you're overweight or obese (with a body mass index [BMI] over 25), you may have lower blood folate levels than smaller women, according to one study. Overweight women's babies also have a higher rate of neural tube defects . . . and although it's still unclear what the connection is between weight, lower folate levels, and NTDs, it doesn't hurt to start taking 1,000 mcg folic acid in a supplement form before you conceive and keep it up through pregnancy. . . .

Should I take a supplement? Definitely. If you're like most people, you don't get the amount of folate you need from your diet, and research shows that the body actually absorbs the synthetic version of this vitamin (found in supplements and enriched foods) much better than the version that occurs naturally in certain foods. On the days you can't stomach your prenatal vitamin in early pregnancy, at least take a separate folic acid supplement [BabyCenter, n.d.].

3B. In new pairs, prepare a day's diet (providing 600–800 mcg. folic acid) for your friend who is pregnant. We'll hear a sample.

Learning Task 4: Who Needs to Know This? And How!

4A. In pairs, list the items from this short introductory session that you want to share with friends. We'll hear all that's on your list.

4B. In pairs, decide one way you might get this news out. Make a poster, an advertisement, or a TV or radio public service announcement that will help other women know about folic acid. We'll share your creative ideas.

Notice that there are two hundred women in a lecture hall, and no lecture. However, there was significant input—the reading they did, which could be on handouts or on the PowerPoint slide projection. The important distinction in this dialogue education "lecture" is that all of the women were working with the new content for the whole time. The design made that happen. Notice that the first learning task involved what might be happening with real people, the second involved learners' doing something with a set of input from the CDC, and the third offered new input for a different stage of life. The fourth learning task invites them to take it back home—to their friends.

Choices: Seniors' Health Care Resources

Senior resources in my North Carolina county are available, but information about them is not as accessible as it might be. An adult education course on these resources often consists of an illustrated lecture by a representative of Resources for Seniors (formerly The Council on Aging) using PowerPoint. When seniors become ill, they and their family depend on a hospital social worker to describe their choices. This short course is addressed to healthy seniors who can make early choices, knowing the diverse resources that are theirs. This is an example of a dialogue education design, with learning tasks for one of the six course sessions.

Who? (The participants)

A group of twenty to thirty senior men and women who come to a local senior center. They range in age from sixty-five to one hundred!

Why? (The situation)

As health issues emerge, these seniors are faced with choices about housing and health care. Resources for Seniors has documented rich resources on the Internet. These seniors need to know about these resources so they can make informed choices.

When? (The time frame)

One hour a week for six weeks (six hours).

Where? (The site)

A comfortable room at the senior center; a computer with internet access on a desk; tables for six.

What? (The content)

- Resources for seniors.
- Resources for home care.
- Resources for housing.
- Resources for long-term care.
- Resources for retirement care.
- Support groups.
- In-home companions.
- Facility-based respite options.

What for? (Achievement-based objectives)

By the end of this six-week program, all participants will have

- Identified Resources for Seniors (RFS).
- Examined resources for home care; used the resource.
- Examined resources for housing; used the resource.
- Examined resources for long-term care; used the resource.
- Examined resources for retirement care; used the resource.
- Reviewed a list of support groups; named ways these can be helpful.
- Reviewed the list of in-home companions; added to the suggestions.
- Examined facility-based respite options; selected one.

How? (Learning tasks and materials)

Session One

Learning Task 1: The Council on Aging—Resources for Seniors
Read over this mission statement of Resources for Seniors. Circle what is important to you now in this mission statement. We'll hear what you circled.

Resources for Seniors, Inc. (RFS) of Wake County, North Carolina, was founded in 1973. Our mission is to provide home and community based services so that disabled and senior adults can maximize their independence for as long as possible while remaining in their homes. We are committed to excellence in service and care for individuals, families, and their communities. In 1993 the name of the agency was changed from Council on Aging of Wake County to better describe our guiding mission. We continue to serve as the Council on Aging of Wake County [Resources for Seniors, n.d.].

Learning Task 2: Home Care Resources—Levels of Home Care

2A. At your table, describe a situation you know of in which someone in your family or a neighbor has had home health care. What struck you about the service? We'll hear a sample.

2B. Read over this excerpt from the RFS website. Circle what is important to you at this time. We'll hear all you circled.

Homemakers or companions can provide assistance with meal preparation, light housekeeping, laundry, errands, and other "hands-off" tasks. If the client only needs supervision or a "sitter," this may be the appropriate level. Some home care agencies offer these services in addition to more complex services—look for the @ next to the agency name below. There are also specialized agencies that provide only companion-level services—see last page.

Home health aides or certified nursing assistants (CNAs) can, in addition to the services provided by homemakers, assist with "hands-on" personal care needs such as bathing, dressing, walking, and toileting. CNAs cannot give injections or dispense medications, though they can remind the patient to take their medication.

Skilled nursing and other skilled services such as physical therapy, occupational therapy, speech therapy, and medical social services are also offered by many home health agencies. [Resources for Seniors, n.d.]

Learning Task 3: Paying for Home Health Care

Read over the excerpt from the RFS website on payment options. Circle what is important to you and what you need to question. We'll hear all that you circled.

Medicare provides a limited Home Health Benefit which may be available to patients following certain illnesses and injuries. It does not require prior hospitalization. Medicare pays for home health visits under the following circumstances:

1. The patient must need intermittent skilled nursing or therapies as well as personal care,

2. The patient must be homebound,

3. The care must be ordered by and under the direction of a physician, and

4. The agency must be certified to provide Medicare visits.

If all these conditions are met, a home health aide approved for Medicare Home Health can assist with personal care on a limited basis (often only 1–2 hours per visit). Medicare covers the cost of this service, however this benefit is usually time-limited and is discontinued if and when the patient no longer needs skilled nursing or therapies.

Medicaid also pays for home health aides for people who need help with personal care, under a program called PCS (Personal Care Services). To receive this benefit, the patient must have Medicaid, the service must be recommended by a physician, and the agency must be Medicaid-certified and provide PCS services. PCS covers only a small number of hours of care per week (max. 60 hours per month), and must include help with personal care needs such as bathing. PCS cannot serve clients who only need homemaker services such as housekeeping and meal preparation.

Medicaid also offers the CAP (Community Alternatives Program) to help older and disabled adults remain in community settings rather than being placed in nursing homes. This program is for people who have low income and assets, and who are at risk of nursing home placement because of their care needs. For patients who qualify, CAP can provide extensive home-based services.

Private Pay: Some agencies also provide services of nurses or home health aides which can be paid for privately by the patient. These services are called private duty services [Resources for Seniors, n.d.].

Learning Task 4: Hospice

4A. At your table, describe an experience you have had with hospice in your family or with friends. We'll hear a small sample.

4B. Read over this excerpt from the website of RFS. Circle what is useful to you now.

Hospice services provide pain relief, symptom management, and supportive care for persons with limited life expectancy as determined by a physician. Medicare and other insurance will pay for hospice services. Nonprofit hospice agencies may commit to provide services even if the patient can't pay [Resources for Seniors, n.d.].

4C. Listen to a presentation from a representative of Hospice of Wake County. What are your questions?

Learning Task 5: Application and Integration

Read this case study. Considering what you have learned today, decide at your table what health care services Patrick should get. We'll hear a sample.

Patrick's Dilemma. Patrick is a seventy-year-old former teacher. He lives alone in his home which he owns in Raleigh, North Carolina. Patrick has had open-heart surgery to replace a leaking valve. His prognosis is very good. He wants to live at home while recuperating. His brother will be with him for a few weeks. Patrick's income is from Social Security and interest from savings. He is not Medicaid eligible. He has need of intermittent skilled nursing care and physical therapy as well as personal care. His physician has ordered nursing care and physical therapy. He will be homebound for at least two months.

The seniors are invited to attend session two on housing on the following Friday.

These three examples show something of the accountability of dialogue education designs in health care situations: in community health education, in hospital staff development, in university courses. Myriad opportunities arise for careful design and teaching so that men and women of all ages learn what they need to know to preserve and protect their own health and the health of their children.

15

DIALOGUE EDUCATION IN A COLLEGE CLASSROOM

Pray for doubt.

When college and university teachers want to design for learning, and not only for excellent teaching, they can look to the principles and practices of dialogue education for support.

Learning Needs and Resources Assessment

Prior to designing the final draft of an undergraduate or graduate course, you as professor can obtain the e-mail addresses of a significant sample of those registered for your course. You can invite input from these learners on the draft design of the course, their purpose for taking such a course, and their hopes for learning. This is a sample e-survey:

> I am Professor Jane Vella. I am pleased that you are taking History 297 *The History of East Africa in the Twentieth Century*. You can help me by replying to these questions in a short e-mail before January 15:
>
> Having read the attached draft design for the course, what are your questions or responses?
>
> Why are you personally taking this course?
>
> Name one or two expectations you have for this course.
>
> I am sending this e-mail to twenty randomly selected students registered for this course. If you have questions, about this process, please call me at . . .

Alternately, you can invite a focus group to your office to respond orally to the same set of questions. You can invite students to a potluck supper or a tea and elicit informal responses to such questions. However creatively you do it, the responses you get will inform, not form your course, and will begin a sound relationship not only with the focus group, but with the entire class, who will have gained a sense that you, the professor, are listening to them.

Safety

On the first day of class, safety is established. If an LNRA of sorts has been used, students are curious, if not reassured. How can you as professor establish safety? First, you can set out the parameters of the course explicitly and unambiguously. What is a student portfolio? How is it graded? What is meant by student presentations? In a sense, safety is a corollary of clarity of expectations and mutual responsibilities.

Safety is the *sine qua non* of learning; it has nothing to do with the depth and intensity of the challenge the content offers students. When reviewing a chemistry course outline that includes as a *What for?* (achievement-based objective) "You will have *memorized* the periodic table: elements, symbols, atomic weights," they can see their work is cut out for them. There is no discussion of what the content of the course is, or of the sequence of that content. That is established by professional standards. There may be rich dialogue in an initial learning task on the significance of that content to this group of young adults, and to their development as professionals.

Safety is in the design; safety is also in the ongoing dialogue: how students are addressed, how questions are answered, how humor is used, how promises are made and kept. A college or university classroom is a sacred place of contract: *I will do this and that, and you will do this and that, and we will all learn.*

Although graduate or undergraduate courses may indeed prepare young people (and older students too) for the workplace, they are not *training* for that workplace. A university course is first of all a *learning* place, where an individual's boundaries—cognitive, affective, and kinesthetic—are stretched.

The student can experience in such a learning place the kindness, attention, teamwork and mutuality, supportive challenge and safety that enables deep learning. Safety in a college classroom is always the other side of the coin of challenge. It is never the easy way. In your discipline, in your classroom, safety and challenge will emerge in your idiosyncratic mode.

Sound Relationships

The scale of college teaching is often an obstacle to the establishment of the kind of relationship that affects learning. A history class with five hundred freshman students is intimidating to professor and students alike.

However, this principle holds: adult learners need the safety of a sound relationship in order to courageously face the challenge of complex learning.

Your effort to do a needs assessment and to create systems for safety will speak to students. Name tents or name tags will help. Your own creativity will produce the systems that are appropriate in your unique university or college.

As teaching assistants support small-group sessions after a large-scale lecture in many schools, so these young student-teachers can be taught the importance of their relationship to those in their group. You can urge them to do simple things that build sound relationships:

- Address students by their name.
- Respond politely to all questions.
- Share resources such as useful URLs and your own e-mail address.
- Invite students to form small support groups.

- Set team learning tasks.
- Keep office appointments.
- Mark papers with creative respect.

Sequence and Reinforcement

This principle and practice begins at the outset of a college course, when students see the course outline or curriculum. The sequence must be visible, and the occasions of reinforcement transparent. Sequence of content is paired with a reasonable sequence in the process as it moves from simple to more complex, from short to longer work expectations, from basic to advanced procedures, from group work to solo presentations.

A clear, unambiguous course outline adds to the safety that students feel as they move into uncharted waters. Sequence supports safety, which supports students' ability to take on tough learning challenges.

Reinforcement also involves content and process. University classes can open with a review of last week's work and a question period about that learned content. This segues into the content and process of the moment.

Praxis

A college course that uses praxis as its backbone is teaching both the content of the discipline and how to learn new content as it emerges explosively day by day. Praxis means action with reflection. The action in a history course might be having read a chapter in the text, or seen a film depicting a moment in history, or listened to a panelist's opinions on the subject. The learning task—the praxis—will invite all students to interpret, to empathize, to argue or oppose the position offered; to reflect personally on the content in such a way that both they and the content are transformed.

In this twenty-first century, the way we teach is changing in laboratories or research centers *as we teach it*. Only praxis will prepare university students to continue learning, interpreting, judging, reflecting. Praxis must become a habit of mind and a habit of action (with reflection).

The sequence of four elements of a learning task—inductive work connecting content to students' context, input offering new content, implementation inviting students to do something with the new content, and integration asking them to take new content home—is praxis. And praxis in a university classroom is learning.

Subjects: Learners as Decision Makers

How can you, a college professor, see students in your courses as decision makers? And how can that perception be visible to the students? You have invited their review of the course outline in the LNRA; you have set up systems for safety and sound relationships among them and with them; you have demonstrated a process that involves their cooperation and engagement and demands much hard work. They are already making the decision to stay in your course. They are deciding with whom they will work in a small group, how much work to do, and how much initiative to take. They are beginning to feel the terror and joy of being subjects or decision makers of their own learning. They are sharing their excitement about learning with their peers. Jane Marantz Connor describes such an experience of teaching in her contributive chapter "Dialogue Education Goes to College," which opens *Dialogue Education at Work* (Vella and Associates, 2004).

Research on dialogue education often comes from the field of adult education. Fewer examples come from traditional higher education settings. There are many reasons why professors are reluctant to give up the standard monologue lecture format, including peer pressure, reward structures that discourage expenditures of effort in developing a new pedagogy, and student expectations. I have learned that what you do in a small class you can do in a large class; it just requires more planning and attention to details. The psychology course Dr. Connor taught at State University of New York grew in three years from thirty-five students to an enrollment of 419. The transformational character of this course does not appear to have been affected by the very large increase in numbers (Vella and Associates, 2004).

Ideas, Feelings, and Actions

Every class in a learning-centered dialogue education college classroom involves all three of these epistemological elements: ideas (cognitive work), feelings (affective considerations), and actions (kinesthetic learning). The classes involve and engage college students in learning tasks that demand all of their energy. In a history course, they are charged to respond to a chapter in a textbook or to a lecture by designing a poster that refutes or accepts the facts of the lecture or the chapter; they are invited to use the Internet to discover current research on the topic; they can Skype a friend in a nearby university to discover what the friend is learning about this issue. As small groups report on their implementation tasks, a wider and deeper research agenda develops that may involve naming relevant films or chapters in other texts that come from differing perspectives. Such research becomes the agenda for the week. This pattern of learning can occur in every college classroom: biology, information technology, psychology, sociology, chemistry, political science. There is a World Wide Web of resources that manifests the interconnectedness of various research agenda.

As we saw in "On Learning" in the Preface, learning (cognitive, affective, and psychomotor) takes place in the small group during the college class; transfer occurs as further research is done, experiments are completed, and papers are written after the class. The impact of such learning and transfer is the purpose of your course: the development of a competent professional lawyer, or physician, or university professor, or artist.

Immediacy

Design and teach your college courses using the principles and practices named so far, and you will see the usefulness of immediacy: content meeting context in a fruitful encounter of learning and transfer. History classes speak to current political debates, graduate courses in theology address moral dilemmas faced by students and their families, biology experiments relate to the physical development of students' young children. The principle of immediacy invites you to connect content to their context, which you know and have studied through the LNRA and the continuing dialogue of the classroom. Again I think of the novelist E. M. Forster, who gave us this cogent pedagogical axiom: "Only connect."

New Roles for Dialogue

As university professors all over the world have been discovering, dialogue education brings you, the teacher, to a new role. You are no longer the only knower in the room, the only person at the point of power, the transmitter of facts and figures. Now you are listener, designer, researcher, knowledgeable resource, teacher, learner, coach, and judge.

In lieu of standing at a lectern and brilliantly presenting content gleaned from myriad sources, you design sessions that open those sources to the students. You present content as hypothetical, not as determined, and you invite the tough learning that science demands, asking students to turn that content into sound theory that will work in their context. Your new role merges the lecture hall and the laboratory to make learning occur at a new level of critical thinking. Students connect to the content and to you as they are compelled to listen, reflect, judge, rewrite, and compose what they are learning.

Engagement

An engaged college class may look a bit unruly and sound a bit noisy as small groups work with a difficult chapter to distill major concepts and prepare an outline. At other times, deeply engaged students may be quiet, reflecting or working out a problem alone or together. They may be on a search engine or another internet site doing research; they may be communicating with an astronaut or the CEO of a Fortune 500 company. A well-conceived learning task focuses such engagement on a particular learning, selected by the professor. The timing of the task is such that pressure is brought to bear to complete the research, finish the task, and ensure the learning.

Being present at such engagement is being in a sacred space. I have felt my breath drawn from my body (aha!) in classrooms where graduate students were so engaged. Can this occur day after day, in course after course? You, good reader, are the only one who can respond to that question.

Teamwork

A learning task is an open question put to a small group, with all the resources they need to respond. However you design your college classes, using these principles and practices will invite you to put students into learning teams—small groups where they share their grasp of a lecture, their questions, the implications they perceive from their unique context, and their objections. What they share is determined by your open question (learning task). The small group becomes the mini-class in a larger classroom or lecture hall. It is the place of learning. Small groups can be pairs, or threes, or, in a properly equipped dialogue education setting, a table for four to six.

The sequence and reinforcement in small-group work moves from broad questions that involve all working together to more precise work that demands individual responses. The group does not learn; individuals learn in a group. Such learning may be seen as transfer as a group takes action integrating learning into life after the class. But learning is always individual and idiosyncratic.

Accountability

The individual student is responsible for his learning, accountable to himself and to his family and peers. The teacher is accountable for having designed a college class at undergraduate or graduate level that will end in accountable learning. The very design is accountable. How do the learners know they know? They just did something significant with the content, and documented what they did in such a way that there is solid evidence of learning. Such evidence or indicators of learning can be a physical product: a map, timeline, or poster; a tape of a language session; a video; or a written paragraph. These indicators can be collated in a personal portfolio that is available for review at any time.

This is not a notebook, with the professor's lecture summarized. This is not a set of quizzes or tests, checking memory. This is a portfolio of evidence of constructed learning—the results of accumulated learning tasks. The portfolio can have a section on transfer, to which synthesis papers or advanced research are added. A growing annotated bibliography is an example of transfer, as students select from the course bibliography those titles relevant to their interests and context. Accountability is the beginning and the end of the process: a professor assumes a willingness to work and to be accountable on the part of all who take her course, and the students assume that she will move them relentlessly to the knowledge, skills, and attitudes projected in her course outline. The mutual accountability is a contract between consenting adults who are determined to learn and to teach.

Respect

Dialogue education in a college classroom will be marked by mutual respect. The professor shows respect for her students by her assiduous preparation and careful attention to their work. Students in small-group work are compelled by the design to collaborate and learn together.

I hear on my back porch horror stories of drugs, insane violence, and guns on campus, disrespect and antagonism to those who are "different." Respect in dialogue education is an inclusive principle. No one can exclude himself; no one will be excluded.

This principle (and practice) of respect assumes that everyone in a college classroom has something to offer and something to learn. As we design, using these principles and practices, the ultimate respect is offered to the knowledge itself and to nature, whose mysteries unfold to our efforts to give us, alone and together, the deepest joy.

Epilogue

It is my hope that this book makes clear the political implications of dialogue education. The basic relationship of teacher and learners is transformed. Paulo Freire describes the new relationship:

> Through dialogue, the teacher-of-the-students and the students-of-the-teacher cease to exist and a new term emerges: teacher-student with student-teachers. The teacher is no longer merely the one who teaches, but one who is himself taught in dialogue with the students, who in turn while being taught also teach. They become jointly responsible for a process in which all grow [1972, p. 67].

This is what the design of dialogue education makes happen. This is what Freire calls "education as the practice of freedom" and what I call the practice of peace.

In my understanding of this educational method, the means is dialogue, the end is learning, and the purpose is peace.

Appendix A

GLOSSARY OF TERMS USED IN DIALOGUE EDUCATION

Achievement-based objective (ABO)   Teaching and learning objectives established using the future perfect tense: "By the end of this hour, all will have . . ."

Each achievement-based objective relates to its corollary content piece and, in fact, is a *contract* with the learner that the learning task will work to teach that content.

Axioms   The axioms of dialogue education are significant and playful:

> Pray for doubt.
>
> Don't tell what you can ask; don't ask if you know the answer; tell in dialogue.
>
> A learning task is a task for the learner.
>
> See this growing list at www.globalearning.com

Congruence   This principle maintains that because we teach the way we were taught, and we learn as much from what we see done as from what is said, we must do what we are teaching others to do. It is as simple as that, and as demanding.

Consultative voice   The consultative voice *suggests:* "How about?" Compare with the *deliberative voice*.

Content   What we are teaching in a given time period; the *What?* of the seven design steps. Content can be cognitive material, affective materials, or kinesthetic material—physical skills; that is, content can be ideas, feelings, or actions.

Deliberative voice   The deliberative voice decides (compare with *consultative* voice). Clarity about this distinction is one of the best management tools.

Design   What we call a lesson plan in dialogue education. It is well-structured by the seven design steps, thoroughly considered in every aspect, and flexible to change as the need arises. A well-constructed design ensures learning; it is the basis of accountability.

Dialogue   Paulo Freire taught us the importance of dialogue in adult education. The word comes from the Greek *dia*: between and *logos*: the word, so it means *the word between us*. The dialogue in dialogue education is not between the teacher and the learners, but among learners, of whom the teacher is one.

Impact   The difference or change that occurs in a person or an organization as a function of a learning event or a series of learning events.

Implementation   The third of four elements of a learning task, in which learners do something with the new content in order to learn it or to change it, as the case may be. This is the element in which the learner applies the new learning.

Indicators   In dialogue education, the behaviors that show learning or transfer or impact. Indicators are finely delineated behavioral outcomes.

Inductive work   The first of four elements of a learning task, in which the learner and the new content meet in the learner's context. *Induction* means moving from the particular or specific to the general. Inductive work in a learning task anchors the new content in the life and experience of learners.

Input   The second of four elements of a learning task: the delivery of new content, research-based, current, significant, accessible, visually supported. This is where new content is added, through infinite modes: an illustrated lecture, a reading, a PowerPoint presentation, a visit to a website, a panel of experts. The mode is determined by the learning context, which begins with the *Who?*—the learners.

Integration   The fourth of four elements of a learning task, bringing the learning home (away) into the lives of learners. Notice that it ends where it began—in the context of learners.

Language   The very language of dialogue education is structured for graciousness and respect. In lieu of *I want you to . . .* a professor says *The next learning task is to . . .* Learners are called by name (name tags, name tents on desks); the participants say *please* and *thank you.* The language of dialogue education is a metaphor of the tone of dialogue.

Learning   The end of it all. Learning is what occurs during the event, and achievement-based objectives are designed to ensure this.

Learning needs and resources assessment (LNRA)   A vital step in the preparation of a learning design. We ask questions of or study or observe the learners in their context to gain an understanding of that context and of their purpose in doing this learning.

Learning task   An open question put to a small group, with all the resources they need to respond. Learning tasks have four elements: (1) inductive work, anchoring the new content in the learners' context; (2) input, the new content presented; (3) implementation, in which learners do something with the new content applying it; and (4) integration, bringing the new content home.

Materials   Learning materials are vital to dialogue education. They must be congruent with our purpose and our process. That is, we expect them to be accessible, full of current and significant research, aesthetic, and well-composed. Learning materials include print and electronic matter.

Podcast   A lesson offered on the Internet for access 24/7 around the world. See http://www.globalearning.com/podcasts.htm for lessons and dialogues on all of the content of this book.

Portfolio   A portfolio of students' work serves as a set of written indicators that are congruent with the behavioral indicators of learning and transfer. This is one mode of documentation toward evaluation.

Principles and practices   A growing list that began with twelve named in *Learning to Listen, Learning to Teach* (Vella, 2002). The original twelve are learning needs and resources assessment, accountability, respect for the learner as subject, engagement, immediacy, a new role for the professor, sound relationships, safety, praxis: action with reflection, sequence, ideas/feeling/actions, and teamwork. Dialogue is obviously a paramount principle and practice, and congruence with all of these is another.

Quantum thinking   A way of perceiving the world based on principles—synchronicity, the whole is more than the sum of its parts, interrelatedness—that have emerged from research in quantum physics (see Vella, 2002).

Resistance   Behavior on the part of learners who do not want to learn the given content or do not want to join the collaborative process. Meeting resistance without destroying the purpose of an educational venture is a challenge that demands the use of all of the principles and practices, especially respect, listening, and the use of the deliberative voice.

Seven steps of design   These seven steps in sequence are the planning tool of dialogue education: the *Who?* and *Why?* the *When?* and *Where?* the *What?* and *What for?* and the *How?* The *Who?* includes learners and teachers. The *Why?* is the situation that demands this learning. The *When?* is the time frame. The *Where?* is the site. The *What?* is the content. The *What for?* is the achievement-based objectives that correlate to the content, and the *How?* is the learning tasks and materials.

Site The site of learning (the *Where?* in the seven design steps) is an important condition that can serve or obstruct learning. Configuring and structuring the site to serve learning is an important role of the professor.

Small group The true site of learning in dialogue education, where learners struggle together with new content and make it their own in a valid, honest way.

Structure Dialogue education is a structured system. Some of the structures are the learning task, the seven design steps, the LNRA, evaluation indicators, and the principles and practices at work. Structure is a means to evoke spontaneity and creativity.

Synthesis A synthesis task puts a series of tasks all together. It often falls at the end of a day or a series of learning tasks.

Time frame The *When?* in the seven design steps is exact and well-considered. It is the amount of time learners have in a session. When designating the time to complete a learning task, the dialogue educator uses "We'll share our work at 2:00 PM" rather than "I will give you ten minutes to complete this task."

Transfer The use of new learning in a new context, after the learning event. Indicators of transfer are behavioral evidence that cognitive, affective, or psychomotor (kinesthetic) learning has taken place.

Verbs for learning tasks The verb in a learning task indicates what the learners will do to learn the new content, to document their learning, to develop a product that offers solid quantitative evidence of learning. (See Appendix B for a set of these verbs.)

Visuals Visual support is important to adult learning. Visuals must be large and accessible, in language that serves learning, with illustrations that are respectful of the learners' culture. A picture is worth a thousand words. Visuals can also serve an aesthetic purpose.

Appendix B

TOUGH VERBS FOR LEARNING TASKS

These verbs are precise and specific. They demand engagement of learners and can lead to meaningful products that, in turn, can be indicators of learning.

described	constructed	interviewed
lifted	measured	danced
reconstructed	graphed	adjusted
painted	critiqued	built
prepared	prioritized	itemized
cooked	numbered	sorted
established	extended	drawn
advocated	argued	debated
examined	labeled	balanced
summed up	compiled	advised
estimated	measured	composed
revealed	selected	judged
voted	revised	gathered
calculated	posted	timed
formulated	appraised	persuaded
diagrammed	collected	shared
rewritten	blended	outlined
averaged	inspected	combined
highlighted	distributed	compared
chosen	named	modified
inspected	taste-tested	baked

(continued)

eliminated	rearranged	substituted
installed	printed	projected
inserted	weighed	reported
typed	cast	scavenged
reversed	stitched	collated
arranged	displayed	defined
conducted	audited	identified
collected	connected	verified
filled out	requested	toured
analyzed	listed	mapped out
created	inscribed	developed
practiced	acted out	played
extracted	rephrased	abbreviated

References

Anheuser-Busch. *Family Talk: How to Talk with Your Kids About Drinking: A Guide for Parents.* St. Louis, Mo.: Anheuser-Busch, 2005.

BabyCenter, n.d. "Folic Acid: An Important Way to Prevent Birth Defects." [http://www.babycenter.com/refcap/476.html].

Belenky, M. F., Bond, L. A., and Weinstock, J. S. *A Tradition That Has No Name: Nurturing the Development of People, Families, and Community.* New York: Basic Books, 1997a.

Belenky, M. F., Clinchy, B. M., Goldberger, N. R., and Tarule, J. M. *Women's Ways of Knowing: The Development of Self, Voice and Minds* (10th anniversary ed.). New York: Basic Books, 1997b. (Originally published 1986.)

Berardinelli, P. K. "Using Dubin's Theory Building Methodology to Construct a Model of the Impact of Management Training." Doctoral dissertation, North Carolina State University, 1991. *Dissertation Abstracts International,* AAI 91, 233–43.

Berardinelli, P. K., Burrow, J. L., and Dillon-Jones, L. S. "Management Training: An Impact Theory." *Human Resource Development Quarterly,* 6(1) (1950), 79–90.

Bloom, B. S. *Taxonomy of Educational Objectives, Handbook I: The Cognitive Domain.* New York: McKay, 1956.

Bushardt, S. C., and Fowler, A. R. "The Art of Feedback." In J. Gordon (ed.), *Classic Activities for Building Better Teams.* Hoboken, N.J.: Wiley, 2003.

Collins, J. *Good to Great: Why Some Companies Make the Leap—and Others Don't.* New York: HarperBusiness, 2001.

Conrad, R. M., and Donaldson, J. A. *Engaging the Online Learner: Activities and Resources for Creative Instruction* (Online Teaching and Learning Series). San Francisco: Jossey-Bass, 2004.

Davis, B. G. *Tools for Teaching.* San Francisco: Jossey-Bass, 1993.

Dewey, J. *Experience and Education.* New York: Collier Books, 1963. (Originally published 1938.)

Dick, W., and Carey, L. *The Systematic Design of Instruction*. Glenview, Ill.: Scott, Foresman, 1985.

Edwards, B. *The New Drawing on the Right Side of the Brain*. New York: Tarcher/Putnam, 1999.

Finkelstein, J. *Learning in Real Time: Synchronous Teaching and Learning Online*. San Francisco: Jossey-Bass, 2006.

Francis, D., and Young, D. *Improving Work Groups*. Hoboken, N.J.: Wiley, 2001.

Freire, P. *Pedagogy of the Oppressed*. New York: Herder and Herder, 1972.

Hatch, T. *Into the Classroom: Developing the Scholarship of Teaching and Learning*. San Francisco: Jossey-Bass, 2005.

Hutchinson, T. "Community Needs Assessment Methodology." Unpublished paper, University of Massachusetts, 1978.

Jung, C. G. Typology Survey. [http://www.humanmetrics.com/].

Kidshealth for Parents. "Folic Acid and Pregnancy." Nemours Foundation, n.d. [http://www.kidshealth.org/parent/pregnancy_newborn/pregnancy/folic_acid.html].

Kiersey, D., and Hatch, M. *Please Understand Me: Character and Temperament Types* (3rd ed.). Del Mar, Calif.: Prometheus Nemesis Books, 1984.

Lewin, K. *Field Theory in Social Science*. New York: Harper Collins, 1951.

Mezirow, J. *Transformative Dimensions of Adult Learning*. San Francisco: Jossey-Bass, 1991.

National Institutes of Health. Just Enough for You: About Food Portions, NIH Publication No. 03-5287, n.d. [http://arthritis.about.com/od/weight/ht/foodportions.htm].

Norris, J. *From Telling to Teaching: A Dialogue Approach to Adult Learning*. North Myrtle Beach, S.C.: Learning by Dialogue, 2003.

Palmer, P. *The Courage to Teach*. San Francisco: Jossey-Bass, 1997.

Paloff, R. M., and Pratt, K. *Building Learning Communities in Cyberspace: Effective Strategies for the Online Classroom*. San Francisco: Jossey-Bass, 1999.

———. *Lessons from the Cyberspace Classroom: The Realities of Online Teaching*. San Francisco: Jossey-Bass, 2001.

———. *Collaborating Online*. San Francisco: Jossey-Bass, 2005.

Polya, G. *How to Solve It: A New Aspect of Mathematical Method*. Princeton, N.J.: Princeton Press, 1945.

Population Growth and Balance. [http://www.arcytech.org/java/population/popintro.html].

Rabinowitz, M., Blumberg, F. C., and Everson, H. T. *The Design of Instruction and Evaluation*. Mahwah, N.J.: Erlbaum, 2004.

Resources for Seniors, n.d. [http://www.resourcesforseniors.com].

Rhoads, D., Dewey, J., and Michie, D. *Mark as Story: An Introduction to the Narrative of a Gospel*. Minneapolis: Fortress Press, 1999.

Roizen, M. F., and Oz, M. C. *You: On a Diet*. New York: Free Press, 2006.

Shelton, C. If You Only Have a Hammer. [http://www.newwork.com/Pages/Contributors/Shelton/Hammer.html]. 1999.

Streibel, B. J., Joiner, B. L., and Scholtes, P. R. *The Team Handbook* (3rd ed.). Madison, Wis.: Oriel, 2003.

Tarrant, H. (ed.). *The Last Days of Socrates* (rev. ed.). New York: Penguin Classics, 2003.

University of Detroit Mercy. Guidelines for Online Teaching. [http://www.comput-ease.net/teaching-learning/discussion.htm].

Vella, J. *Taking Learning to Task*. San Francisco: Jossey-Bass, 2001.

———. *Learning to Listen, Learning to Teach* (2nd ed.). San Francisco: Jossey-Bass, 2002.

Vella, J., and Associates. *Dialogue Education at Work: A Case Book*. San Francisco: Jossey-Bass, 2004.

Vella, J., Berardinelli, P., and Burrow, J. *How Do They Know They Know? Evaluating Adult Learning*. San Francisco: Jossey-Bass, 1997.

Wink, W. *Engaging the Powers: Discernment and Resistance in a World of Domination*. Minneapolis: Fortress Press, 1992.

Zohar, D. *Rewiring the Corporate Brain*. San Francisco: Berrett-Koehler, 1997.

Zohar, D., and Marshall, I. *The Quantum Self: Human Nature and Consciousness Defined by the New Physics*. New York: Morrow, 1990.

Index